JARMAN (all this maddening beauty)
and other plays

JARMAN (all this maddening beauty)
and other plays

Caridad Svich

intellect Bristol, UK / Chicago, USA

First published in the UK in 2016 by
Intellect, The Mill, Parnall Road, Fishponds, Bristol, BS16 3JG, UK

First published in the USA in 2016 by
Intellect, The University of Chicago Press, 1427 E. 60th Street,
Chicago, IL 60637, USA

Copyright © 2016 Intellect Ltd

All rights reserved. No part of this publication may be reproduced, stored in a retrieval system, or transmitted, in any form or by any means, electronic, mechanical, photocopying, recording, or otherwise, without written permission.

A catalogue record for this book is available from the British Library.

Series: Playtext
Series editor: Patrick Duggan
Series ISSN: 1754-0933
Electronic ISSN: 1754-0941

Copy-editor: MPS Technologies
Cover designer: Jane Seymour
Production manager: Amy Rollason
Typesetting: Contentra Technologies

ISBN: 978-1-78320-622-3
ePDF: 978-1-78320-623-0
ePUB: 978-1-78320-624-7

Cover Image: John Moletress, *JARMAN (all this maddening beauty)* in performance and rehearsal. Images copyright 2015 Deyanire Musa. All rights reserved.

JARMAN (all this maddening beauty) copyright 2014 by Caridad Svich
Carthage/Cartagena copyright 2002, 2013 by Caridad Svich
The Orphan Sea copyright 2014 by Caridad Svich
All rights reserved.

In regard to professional and amateur performance, readings, and other enquiries for the three plays in this volume, please contact the author's representative Elaine Devlin at Elaine Devlin Literary, 411 Lafayette Street, 6th Flr, NY, NY 10003 USA. Email: edevlinlit@aol.com or New Dramatists alumni desk, 424 West 44th Street, NY, NY 10036 USA.
Email: newdramatists@newdramatists.org

Printed and bound by Short Run Press, UK

Contents

Beautiful Strangeness: The Plays of Caridad Svich Kevin Brown	1
'When I think of him, I think of angels': Introducing *JARMAN (all this maddening beauty)* Theron Schmidt	15
Performing *JARMAN (all this maddening beauty)* John Moletress	21
JARMAN (all this maddening beauty) Caridad Svich	33
Laying Siege to *Carthage* Pedro de Senna	81
Carthage/Cartagena: when I looked up I looked for something (call it hope) Caridad Svich	99
On the Act of Regarding Another: Some Thoughts on Live Performance, Silence, and Fragility Caridad Svich	133
The Orphan Sea Caridad Svich	143
Notes on Contributors	205

Beautiful Strangeness: The Plays of Caridad Svich

Kevin Brown

An invocation in the opening stanza of Caridad Svich's new play *Carthage/Cartagena* entreats, 'I want to learn a new language, to return the one I lost.' In her 25 years as a professional playwright, Caridad Svich has been inventing a new dramatic language. The three plays in this collection share a poetic structure that revels in a free-flowing sense of character and a recasting of narrative that has come to characterize Svich's work over the last several years.

This book opens with *JARMAN (all this maddening beauty)*, a text inspired by the British filmmaker Derek Jarman (1942–1994). When a budding artist is exposed to the works of Derek Jarman, a common muse descends, inspiring artists young and old with an understanding of beauty and violence that transcends temporal and geographical location. Next up is the play *Carthage/Cartagena: when I looked up I looked for something (call it hope)*. A figure is trafficked in a shipping container, subjected to sexual exploitation, later to escape, transmuting a life of violence, brutality, and war into occasional beauty. In a grotesque juxtaposition familiar in Svich's work, visions of ruin and destruction reverberate across time and space, eventually giving way to pink walls and lemon trees. Closing the trio of plays in this book is *The Orphan Sea*. This script moves in a choral, Dionysian mode of narrative. Three choruses comprise versions of mythological figures, including the Odysseus chorus, (those that cross rivers and seas), the Penelope chorus (those that wait for those who are crossing), and the chorus of the city. The metaphorical structure of the play blinks in and out on several levels, ranging from the romantic, poetic rapture of reunion to a contemplation of the postmodern nausea of isolation. Yet, in the end, our couple is reunited, daring us to dream about the ways that some of the best things in life emerge from ruins. Thus, there is an inherent optimism in the work, a hope that humanity will be one day reunited, despite being separated for so long.

Sailing *The Orphan Sea*

During the fall of 2014, award-winning playwright Caridad Svich was commissioned to write a new play for a world premiere production at the University of Missouri at Columbia. The product of this effort is *The Orphan Sea*, a meditation on the archetypes of Penelope and Odysseus, mythological characters from Homer's *Odyssey*. I had the great honor of directing this play, and working hand-in-hand with the author during its development stage. Svich flew out to Missouri for two two-week periods, once in September 2014 and again for the opening of the play. During that time, Svich and I ran workshops with the newly auditioned cast in order to get the play up on its feet.

The Orphan Sea is unlike any play I have ever encountered. The title of the play is inspired by the words of the late great poet Mahmoud Darwish from his collection *Memory for Forgetfulness*: 'Hallowed be your hands, which, all by themselves, raise mountains from the ruins of the orphaned sea' (Darwish 1995: n.p.). Svich's play, although rooted in classical themes, breaks almost every 'rule' of narrative drama that has ever been derived from Aristotle's work on tragedy. In the promotional materials, Svich writes:

> *The Orphan Sea* is a story of us, here, now, and also of who we were once. It is a story of those that cross rivers and seas and those that wait for them, of a lover who searches for one lost years ago, and of someone called Penelope, who may be waiting for someone called Odysseus. Told in poetry, song, film and dance, *The Orphan Sea* is a dream play for anyone that dares to dream.
> (Svich 2014: personal communication, 21 July)

In terms coined by Friedrich Nietzsche in his famous treatise *The Birth of Tragedy from the Spirit of Music* (1872), this script may be Svich's bravest move to date into a new, choral, Dionysian mode of narrative. The lines of individual characters are not delineated in the script, forcing the director to work out the Apollonian elements of the play in the production process. In addition, like much of Svich's work, the play incorporates media elements and invites a gestural world based on the mode of hybrid dance-theatre.

One of the first things one should consider when either reading or staging one of Svich's plays is that the text does not live on the page, but rather is meant to be embodied. Because of its poetic structure, it is tempting to treat these plays as static, as literature. As we entered rehearsal with Svich and began to explore the text with the actors, it was very important for all of us to see how the words came alive when spoken by actors, and how the emotional content of the play came to live and inhabit their bodies. Svich explains the importance of embodiment in her plays in relation to *Iphigenia Crash Land Falls on the Neon Shell That Was Once Her Heart (a rave fable)* and *Twelve Ophelias (a play with broken songs)*, two of her plays that are often performed professionally and at universities:

> Sometimes when people produce them they opt for a very static and declamatory approach because they think 'classical' somehow, but forget that the work is visceral and that the language of the plays lives in the body. I think that's how the plays invite synesthetic approach to performance without being prescriptive.
> (Svich 2015: personal communication, 28 January)

Instead of telling a linear story from A to Z, *The Orphan Sea* challenges us to piece together fragments from the ruins of Aristotle's *Poetics*. In this way, the play is less of a traditional story and more of a meditation on the archetypes of Penelope and Odysseus. The setting of the play is 'Now. And a memory of times before (mythic time).' In contrast to many plays that are set among the ruins of the ancient Athenian civilization, this play breaks out of the typical ruins-as-tragedy trope to end in a rhapsody of optimism and utopianism. Rather than individual protagonists and antagonists, three choruses share the stage, and dialogue can be interchangeably assigned by the director between multiple actors who each play a version of an archetype.

Experiencing the play, the waves of meaning wash over you. There are many ideas buried in the strata of the play, typical of Svich's geographical texts. Some of the recognizable themes are related to borders, including contemporary preoccupations such as immigration and war, personal categories of identity, and the way that technology isolates us by creating borders between one another, the media dividing humanity into 'us versus them.' These elements swirl in a whirlpool of dramaturgy that includes methods of technological mediation worked into the play to emphasize the themes, such as isolation, division, and reunion. Sometimes these methods are purposefully distancing, but more often are meant to immerse the audience and sweep them up into the world of the play.

Memory Theatre

The plays of Caridad Svich can be thought of as a kind of 'Memory Theatre': an attempt to bring physical form to the memories that haunt her characters. This haunting becomes especially viable in the plays when they are staged, and the audience is invited into the action, participating in an all-enveloping, all-encompassing dance with the ghosts of her neo-mythological characters. In her plays, these memories are collisions between archetypes, sending reverberations through time and space, to the point where they become indistinguishable, interchangeable, and ultimately, obliterated.

New School professor Simon Critchley's book *Memory Theatre* (2014) is a genre-blurring hybrid: part philosophical essay, part memoir, and part novel. For Critchley, Memory Theatre is any work of art that is 'an act of memory – an attempt to reconstruct a place' (Critchley quoted in Fraser 2014: n.p.). In the book, the protagonist (also named Simon Critchley) receives a set of boxes from a late professor friend's estate. In the boxes he finds a set of unpublished treatises about 'Memory Theatre,' a theory about an architectural space in the mind and material world where memories can be stored forever – a space that supposedly contains the sum of all knowledge. Ultimately this project fails, suggesting that any attempt to add up the sum of all memories ultimately produces a kind of obliteration, a Gestaltian implosion of both memory and knowledge.

For example, in *JARMAN (all this maddening beauty)*, the artist, the budding artist and the lover share a stage that is the same physical and emotional space, a space that in performance becomes fluid in time. Characters from different timelines interact and merge, evidenced by Svich's allowance that the script may be performed by one actor playing all of the roles if desired. In the final scene, fragmented text is divided between the artist and the budding artist, an optimistic reverie in response to the obliteration of the artist finding out that he is HIV-positive and going blind.

During the first half of *Carthage/Cartagena*, the action is periodically disrupted by the flow of time in order for one of the protagonists to escape from the circumstances of her captivity by dreaming her favorite memories, regressing to the age of six to remember a time her grandmother made her apricot cake for her birthday. Halfway through the play, a captive girl lands in a 'New Country,' presumably America, and proceeds to drift across the country, where you would think her circumstances would be better. She laments: 'What can be done with this / Lonesome child / Adrift in your backyards / In your fever America / What can be done.' But she is always haunted by the memories of her captivity, literally written on her body: 'bastard remains of the before self inscribed in the body and voice.'

The fault lines between memory and history become especially precarious when Svich takes on topics such as immigration, migration, and displacement. On cultural memory, Critchley writes:

> To live in a non-place where there is no memory is a problem. You know that feeling when you go to the West of the US or to Australia where you think 'why are white people here? What are they doing?' It's preposterous; they're just sitting on the surface of this place: it feels like a place which is the obliteration of another landscape of memory.
>
> (Critchley quoted in Fraser 2014: n.p.)

Carthage/Cartagena contains the same kind of cultural haunting, this time by those who are ripped from their own culture and transplanted without recompense.

In *The Orphan Sea*, the disruption of time and space also comes about through the power of memory, in this case cultural memory, amplified because the entire play takes place simultaneously in mythic time and the present moment. In a play about borders, temporal and geographical constructions are rendered invisible and fluid. Multiple instances of the archetypes of Penelope and Odysseus play out their story, but at the same time the myth is witnessed by representatives of the contemporary moment – the citizens of the city as well as the audience. As the play reaches the final movement, the previously triad chorus merges, becoming one. Eventually, all of the mythic characters fall away, obliterated. Just the actors remain, the last traces of the mechanism of theatre. Critchley explains: 'There is a sense in which the way we enforce remembrance produces obliteration' (Critchley quoted in Fraser 2014: n.p.). So, too, it is in Svich's 'Memory Theatre.'

A similar approach to understanding Svich's work can be found in the article 'Cruel Mercies and Tender Ecstasies' by Tamara Underiner, the introduction to Svich's collection of plays *Instructions for Breathing* (2014). Underiner calls attention to similar aspects of Svich's dramaturgy, in terms of her particular use of time and space. Underiner calls Svich's approach 'Hauntological Realism.' According to Underiner, 'hauntology' is a term coined by post-structuralist Jacques Derrida, which:

takes up where ontology leaves off in its charge to explain the nature of what is. Whereas the latter is preoccupied with being, hauntology privileges what lurks at the borders of being – the ghost, the echo, the revenant, the reverberation – those presences that are here but not here, related to an original source that is dimly discernable and of which they partake, but do not share an identity.

(Underiner 2014: xi)

The use of Derrida's concept of hauntology seems apropos in light of the previous discussion about Svich's work and the convergence of time and space, memory and obliteration. Svich writes: 'I'm interested in the remains of/ghosts of culture, and also the inheritances that are borne and marked in our very bones by these remains' (Svich 2012: 7).

The characters in the three plays in this volume have their own kind of 'hauntings.' In *JARMAN*, time is collapsed as the budding artist is transformed by the influence of the artist who lived and died years before. The protagonists of *Carthage/Cartagena* are haunted by the ghosts of their past. In *The Orphan Sea*, mythological characters haunt people from contemporary times, coexisting in the same world, resurrected from cultural memory. According to Underiner: 'Svich's contribution to US dramaturgy is an expansion of the type of language available to us in order to portray the unspeakable, but still perceptible' (Underiner 2014: xvi).

Uncharted Territories

In a 2009 article in *American Theatre*, Justin Maxwell writes: 'Svich reveals herself as a cartographer of cultural dreamscapes. Each play maps out profoundly different, but profoundly human, terrain. These plays, one might say, are like people we know – different on the surface, but driven by similarly human hearts' (Maxwell 2009: 33). The concept of cartography is another key to understanding the plays of Caridad Svich. Each of the plays in this book, *JARMAN*, *Carthage/Cartagena*, and *The Orphan Sea*, has its own unique geography. That is, the dramaturgical structures that comprise many of Svich's plays can be understood as if one were an explorer discovering a new world. It is almost as if each play is its own microcosm, its own planetary world, its own universe, and competes with its own physical principles and rules for gravity, space, and time, and emotional principles such as love, hope, and forgiveness. As such, it is the task of the audience, reader, actor, or director to chart his or her own path through these undiscovered territories.

Sometimes the geographies in Svich's plays are physical, but sometimes we encounter landscapes that are cultural and emotional as well. In 'Considering Utopia,' the introduction to the edited volume *Envisioning the Americas*, Svich explains:

As a playwright (and in my parallel careers as translator and editor), I find myself constantly negotiating the difficult, complex terrain of utopian desire(s). Much of my writing for the stage in particular addresses the shifting political and emotional fault lines of characters left behind by their societies or caught in the rigid hierarchies of non-utopian states. I write hybrid, Latina/o, Anglo, Black, Creole, Asian, Indigenous, transgender, bi, queer, straight figures who often are not labeled or categorized, and do not want to be either.

(Svich 2011a: 9–10)

On other occasions, the plays turn the explorer into a time traveler as well, rapidly shifting or combining settings from different historical time periods.

Svich writes about the importance of 'landscape' in 'Making Plays', the introduction to *Blasted Heavens* (2012). She writes:

My plays, are often, but not always, set in despoiled landscapes composed of fragments of specifically rooted but consciously blurred geographies and multiple historical time frames that bleed into each other to create a savage, salvaged world: a world of transformation and healing, rising out of, but not always, cruelty, and violence.

(Svich 2012: 6–7)

She expands on this theme in her 2009 article about her teacher and mentor, 'The Legacy of Maria Irene Fornes:'

[I]n *Language and Theatre*, Elinor Fuchs and Una Chaudhuri speak eloquently about the way many of the 'language playwrights' (Mac Wellman, Suzan-Lori Parks, Ruth Margraff, Matthew Maguire, Len Jenkin, Erik Ehn) are truly 'landscape playwrights.' Their use of language is topographical, expansive, physical, and demands embodiment in a different manner than say, the work of more 'interior' playwrights like Christopher Shinn, Rebecca Gilman, Neil LaBute, and so forth.

(Svich 2009: 3)

Although not traditionally named in criticism surrounding the so-called 'landscape' playwrights, Svich's writing betrays a heavy influence thereof. Language is mastered through the straightforward use of poetry as playtext, the clarity of her prose, and the resonance and beauty of her words and phrasings. But the words, the language, and the script have a topographical quality as well; thus, language and landscape converge.

For example, the topography of *JARMAN* is dense. It is episodic in structure, which is one quality that all three plays in this volume share. Also, in all these three plays, the text is not delineated according to character. Even though the artist, the budding artist, the lover, and the muse are presumably different characters, Svich makes it clear that these characters do not need to be played by different actors. The beginning stage directions to the play mention the character delineation almost as an afterthought, in a block of text in lower-case letters, as if to say, 'this is not really that important.' The result is that identity and differentiation in Svich's plays often bleed into one another, individual voices becoming multiple, choral. Occasionally, more than one voice emerges from the text, even if there is only one actor speaking. The structure of the play also allows for this de-emphasis of character because each episode is short enough that the only signal to the reader is a short note at the top of each new section as to who is speaking. The way that this shift in identity is signaled to the audience is up to the director of the production.

A radical shift in *JARMAN* is encountered when the budding artist gets a copy of Jarman's film, *The Last of England* (1987). The play chugs along rhythmically up to this point, but then the budding artist describes how, rather than watching the film, 'The promise of sex, drink and / Burning like a Roman candle across the night fills me.' Instead, he goes out on the street to walk to the bar. Along the way he sees smoke and light, what he thinks is a party turns out to be the sight of some sort of massacre, and the structure of the play implodes with the stage directions: '(And then... a montage of word/image...)'. An eruption of text ensues, which may seem to be a free-form of automatic writing that could be lifted from a Joyce novel, but is actually a tribute to the structure of Jarman's films. For the director, the montage becomes an opportunity for media elements to be integrated into the show. If one were to look at the structure of the play as if it were a landscape, geographically, it is the play's fault line.

Similar fault lines exist in the other plays in this book. In *Carthage/Cartagena*, the play is divided into two halves along the moment of the arrival of a passenger to the 'New Country.' Temporal details become compressed. At different moments, the play jumps between the present time and the historical siege of the ancient city of Carthage by Roman soldiers. The result is a realization that the themes and issues raised in the play are timeless. They are as old as humanity itself. In *The Orphan Sea*, the first half of the play is spent in tension, as the Penelopes of the play wait for their Odysseuses to return from war and adventure. The structure of the play then shifts drastically as the men return from the war halfway through the play. The second half of the play evens out and becomes the story of what happens after the couple is reunited. While the characters are archetypes from ancient mythology, anachronism eventually creeps in with references to Google Maps and the world of wires that keeps us alienated from each other in our never-ending quest for 'access.'

Carthage/Cartagena is subtitled *when I looked up I looked for something (call it hope). Ten cantos and a prayer for performance.* Thus, like *JARMAN* and *The Orphan Sea*, the play is structured episodically, in this case in 'cantos,' or songs. The variation comes in the fluctuations in the length of the cantos and the way that the play is bookended by the short prayer: 'Man / Dreams himself heaven / he says / stars / can I speak?' Some cantos are very short (Cantos Five and Six comprise roughly one-third of the entire play), while some cantos are only a few lines.

Another cartological oddity, which has been used in Svich's plays to varying degrees, is that she sometimes uses layout of the play script page to delineate the poetics of the performance. For example, Svich sometimes adds breaks (long pauses) into her plays, which are often marked by an ellipsis '…'. Sometimes she also adds 'shifts.' In *JARMAN*: '//' in the text indicates a slight shift/turn emotionally. In *Carthage/Cartagena*, Svich often employs a unique convention in which, although most of the text is formatted as justified left, she formats some text as justified right. The result is that the text is still not delineated in terms of what character is speaking, at least not in the traditional way. Svich explains, 'In *Carthage* the right justified text is meant as vocal counterpoint [...] my way of notating contrapuntal text' (Svich 2015: personal communication, 28 January). The result of Svich's formatting is her own stamp of kind of new poesies, adding an additional voice to the dialogue, in the same way that Aeschylus is said to have added the second actor to Thespis' first.

The dramaturgical landscape of *The Orphan Sea* has its own oddities, as well as pleasant familiarities. Like *JARMAN* and *Carthage/Cartagena*, the basis of the structure is episodic. The play is essentially 43 short episodes. Each is one to a couple of pages in length. The setting of the play is itself a topography: 'a fluid space, one that can evoke river, road, city, ice floe and a rock in the middle of the ocean.' The particular shape of the play will also be informed by the level of mediation used in each production. Although the use of technology in the staging of this play is not a requirement, certain episodes are noted as possible places where voiceover, film, montage, and dance sequences might occur within the flow of the play. This technological aspect of production is also present in the filmic/montage and 'hidden track' sections of *JARMAN* and *Carthage/Cartagena*.

Neo-Radical Naivety

In a world where everything seems to be increasingly regarded as 'radical,' how does one achieve what is rapidly becoming a sort of 'radical norm?' Svich discusses what it means for theatre to be radical in 'Popular Forms for a Radical Theatre,' the introduction for the edited volume of the same name (2011b). Svich identifies a trend among theatre practitioners at the beginning of the twenty-first century when, in response to negative perceptions of avant-garde theatre as a form that holds contempt for the audience, these artists begin to experiment with popular forms: '[T]heatre artists are pulling apart and/or resurrecting old forms of popular entertainment to tell stories anew in a provocative manner, and thus reawaken the radical impulse in performance' (Svich 2011b: 8). Svich maintains that work does not need to be transgressive in order to be radical. It is possible to create work that challenges and upends tradition without the draining negative energy of that wing of avant-gardists who insist on irony as the dominant artistic tone. Instead, Svich argues:

> Work that ruptures existing traditions, upends convention, brings together disparate energies into cohesion, or markedly shifts the perspective and point of view of an audience and/or witness to a performance event is radical without the necessity of containing material that goes against-the-grain of popular sentiment.
>
> (Svich 2011b: 9)

In 'Exit the Author,' an introductory chapter of Vicky Angelaki's edited volume *Contemporary British Theatre* (2013), Dan Rebellato discusses trends in British playwriting. He notes, '[t]he British theatre's first decade of the twenty-first century began and ended with the death of the author' (Rebellato 2013: 9). The first death was Sarah Kane's suicide, which came closely upon her play *4.48 Psychosis*, which Rebellato calls her 'suicide note.' The death at the end of the decade was of the character Tim Crouch in Tim Crouch's play *The Author*, who slits his throat in a flotation tank. (The stage direction reads 'The death of the author' [Rebellato 2013: 9].) Rebellato bookends the decade with these deaths to make a larger point that the overall trend in playwriting during the last decades of the twentieth and the first decade of the twenty-first century was a removal of the author from their own work, even if that death happened by their own hand.

Rebellato observes strategies developed by several generations of playwrights who began to remove themselves from their work. As evidence, Rebellato offers 'the spread of playtexts that have a new kind of openness' (Rebellato 2013: 15), such as Martin Crimp's *Attempts on Her Life* and Sarah Kane's *4.48 Psychosis* – in both plays neither time nor place is specified, and lines are not assigned to actors. In Mark Ravenhill's *Shoot/Get Treasure/Repeat*, lines either have no character names assigned, or have, according to Ravenhill, the most generic names possible. Simon Stephens' *Pornography* consists of seven sections of text. The script reads: 'This play can be performed by any number of actors. It can be performed in any order.' Caryl Churchill's *Love and Information* is divided into seven sections, scenes can be played in any order, and extra scenes to be inserted are published at the end of the play (Rebellato 2013: 15).

Svich's plays are radical in ways that reflect the dramaturgical strategies that have evolved through these several generations of radical playwrights. In addition to these British playwrights identified by Rebellato, Svich's work can also be seen as another notch on the continuum of several generations of radical American playwrights, such as Ntozake Shange, Suzan Lori-Parks, Paula Vogel, and Sarah Ruhl, whose dramas have challenged the landscape of contemporary drama through radical poetic formations and feminist paradigms, variously in terms of form, style, structure, and content.

Surely, all of the plays in this volume demonstrate a 'new kind of openness' in their content and form. Time and place are fluid in all three plays. The characters in *JARMAN* are named briefly in the opening comments, but not delineated in the text itself. The multi-protagonists (speakers) in *Carthage/Cartagena* are never identified. The reader/audience must scratch beneath the surface of the play to find the true identities of the characters who speak the text of the play. In these plays, there is no 'dialogue' in the way that there is in a traditional play. More of the lines are directed to the audience than other people within the world of the play. In all three plays, the performance is more often (but not always) presentational rather than representational. That is not to say it is declamatory, because the text still must live within the bodies of the actors, but the 'characters' are not impersonated in the same way as they might be in a classical, or even more traditional contemporary play. Svich insists in 'Notes' for *The Orphan Sea*:

Text in the play is not differentiated in regards to specific voices. Sometimes Penelope speaks alone, sometimes with chorus. Sometimes chorus is in unison, sometimes individualized, etc. Decisions regarding this should be made in the rehearsal process and should vary, depending on creative team involved in production.

In addition to an openness in terms of the dramaturgy of plays of this movement, another strategy that Rebellato identifies in a strand among this new wave of playwrights (such as Mike Bartlett, Nick Payne, and Simon Stephens) is 'a turning away from irony […] In some more recent writers, I observe a note of weariness with irony, and instead a self-consciously naive sincerity' (Rebellato 2013: 16). Rebellato calls this turn away from the ironic 'radical naivety.' He explains:

> This tone is so complex because the characters are naive but we are given no reassurance that their authors are any less so. […] Instead, these moments produce a kind of suspension of intentionality, an authorial blankness, where insincerity is banished, but sincerity appears implausible.
>
> (Rebellato 2013: 18)

I would argue that a similar kind of 'radical naivety,' or even 'radical optimism' is found in all three of Svich's plays in this book. Even in a world where radical is the new normal, these plays are exceptionally groundbreaking: politically, formally, and theatrically provocative. Svich's characters are, most of the time, exactly what they appear to be. They say exactly what they mean to say. Although some of the moments in *JARMAN*, *Carthage/Cartagena*, and *The Orphan Sea* are bleak, sometimes desperate and sometimes violent, the overall tone of each of these plays is hopeful. The end of *JARMAN* is a Renaissance tableaux realized in new media. The bookending prayer in *Carthage/Cartagena* calls for a new language, while the chorus in *The Orphan Sea* calls for reparations and community.

José Zayas, director of the Manhattan-based Repertorio Español's production of Svich's play *La Casa de los Espíritus/The House of Spirits*, describes Svich as:

> one of the most intellectually rigorous and linguistically exciting playwrights working in America today. She sees art as a provocation, and her texts are blueprints for creative teams. There is no right way of doing her plays – there is only exploration and transformation.
>
> (Zayas quoted in Maxwell 2009: 33)

This is perhaps what makes Svich's plays truly radical, or maybe even 'neo-radical.' The exact 'geography' of each production will be unique. Depending on the director, *JARMAN* could be done as a one-person-show just as easily as a production with as many as five or more actors. The number of actors in *Carthage/Cartagena* could be equally various. Each new director will need to decide whether they want to tell the story with one individual actor, even as one specific character; or, the play could as easily be interpreted to use multiple actors, or even to use a chorus, as the victim of international sex trafficking is not just one individual in one specific location, but is many and all of its victims. *The Orphan Sea* is multiply choral, and could probably not be done as a one-person-show. However, it could, conceivably, be played with as little as one person in the role of each chorus, up to nine or more actors, total. Beyond questions of casting, decisions as to which actors say which lines, and how the technological elements are incorporated into the production, must be worked out by each new team that takes on the play, each in their own unique way. Even in a world where subversion is the norm, that's pretty radical.

References

Critchley, S. (2014), *Memory Theatre*, London: Fitzcarraldo Editions.

Darwish, M. (1995), *Memory for Forgetfulness: August, Beirut, 1982*, Berkeley: University of California Press, http://ark.cdlib.org/ark:/13030/ft1z09n7g7/. Accessed 24 March 2015.

Fraser, D. (2014), 'Cult of Memory: Simon Critchley Interviewed', *The Quietus*, http://thequietus.com/articles/16607-simon-critchley-memory-theatre-architecture-death-interview/. Accessed 24 March 2015.

Maxwell, J. (2009), 'The Ancient and the Contemporary Collide in the Dreamscapes of Her Plays', *American Theatre*, July/August, pp. 33–35.

Nietzsche, F. (1872), *Die Geburt Der Tragödie/The Birth of Tragedy from the Spirit of Music*, Leipzig: E.W. Fritzsch.

Rebellato, D. (2013), 'Exit the Author', in *Contemporary British Theatre: Breaking New Ground*, V. Angelaki (ed.), New York and London: Palgrave Macmillan, pp. 9–31.

Svich, C. (2009), 'The Legacy of Maria Irene Fornes: A Collection of Impressions and Exercises', *PAJ: A Journal of Performance and Art*, 31: 3, pp. 1–32.

—— (2011a), 'Considering Utopia', in *Envisioning the Americas: Latina/o Theatre & Performance*, C. Svich (ed.), South Gate: NoPassport Press, pp. 5–12.

—— (2011b), 'Popular Forms for a Radical Theatre', in *Popular Forms for a Radical Theatre*, C. Svich and S. Ruhl (eds), South Gate: NoPassport Press, pp. 8–21.

—— (2012), 'Making Plays', in *Blasted Heavens: Five Contemporary Plays Inspired by the Greeks*, C. Svich (ed.), Roskilde: EyeCorner Press, pp. 5–7.

—— (2014), *Instructions for Breathing and Other Plays*, London, New York, Calcutta: Seagull Books.

Underiner, T. (2014), 'Cruel Mercies and Tender Ecstasies', in *Instructions for Breathing and Other Plays*, C. Svich (ed.), London, New York, Calcutta: Seagull Books, pp. vii–xvi.

'When I think of him, I think of angels': Introducing *JARMAN (all this maddening beauty)*

Theron Schmidt

In the parabolic fragments referred to as his 'theses on the philosophy of history,' the messianic thinker Walter Benjamin famously offered a vision of the angel of history, inspired by a painting by Paul Klee: with his face to the past and his back to the future, Benjamin's angel surveys the accumulation of debris of human failure that he would like to repair, but he cannot, for a storm renders his wings useless and blows him ever backward into the future. The storm, Benjamin tells us, is called 'progress.' Angels, saints, and visionaries are everywhere in the luminous films of pioneering artist and activist Derek Jarman. They take the form of polysexual punks in the bedsits of Thatcher's Britain (*The Last of England*, 1987); or stop-framed male bodies entangled in monochromatic landscapes (*The Angelic Conversation*, 1985); or an eroticized early-Christian martyr who would die pierced by innumerable arrows (*Sebastiane*, 1976). Unlike Benjamin's angel, Jarman the filmmaker can move freely across time, creating images that blend historical figures with his present day – and can also freeze time, slowing it down, stretching moments of ecstasy into long, meditative durations. Nor is his gaze horrified by the rubble he sees around him. There is no desire to clean up the broken cities and fractured empires; instead, this is where Jarman's figures bloom, where they fight and fuck and frolic. Maybe he is the reverse of Benjamin's angel; rather than being blown backward away from the past, he looks forward, scattering shattered beauty against which future dreamers will stumble.

Or that, anyway, is the dynamic in Svich's exhilarating, twin-arrowed text, which takes its inspiration from Jarman's life and work. One arc of flight takes the perspective of 'a budding artist' trying to find his own voice long after Jarman's death; he discovers in Jarman's films a quickening electricity that, once embraced, rips its way right through language. The other arrow points forward from the past, taking the form of commentary from Jarman himself as 'the artist' struggling to see his films made. Although there are numerous writings by the 'real' Jarman published in the form of carefully crafted journals (for the filmmaker was always aware of his own self-mythologizing), the words here are imagined by Svich. Somewhere between the two figures is Jarman's lover and muse, a creation imagined by the artist but who will also outlive him. These figures struggle against the times in which they are held. The budding artist, more or less in our own time, has grown up in a supposedly liberated age, but feels himself removed from it. He can speak about 'transgressive objects of desire' (Scene Two, p. 38) and 'the aestheticization of violence' (Scene Two, p. 41), but for him it's just talk, just art-world jargon. Reluctantly introduced to Jarman's films, he is electrified by a 'heartbeatingwonder' (Scene Two, p. 39) that shatters through his shell of irony. Jarman becomes part of his life: 'This artist, whom I have never met, / And who passed away in the late 20th century, / Has become a kind of friend' (Scene Six, p. 55). The Jarman-figure, too, finds companionship in long-dead collaborators: 'I work with Shakespeare, Marlowe, Britten, and Wittgenstein' (Scene Four, p. 48). He is pitched in a culture-war with the rampant consumerism and moral conservativism of 1980s Britain: 'Those bastards can kiss my arse / If they think they're going to poison this country without a fight' (Scene Five, p. 53). Between the two times is suspended a fixed point, one that changed the meaning of Jarman's life and work and that oriented him differently toward his future:

> It is four A.M. on a Sunday
> And I have just learned I am HIV-Positive.
> December 22, 1986.
>
> (Scene Seven, p. 61)

So, two lives, in two times: a kind of angelic conversation, to take the title of one of Jarman's films. But Svich does more than just place these two times against each other as parallel stories. What is extraordinary is the way that the heat of the longing that each feels seems to warp time itself, to rend its fabric and queer its orientation. The budding artist wishes to defer watching his DVD of *The Last of England*, Jarman's 1987 punk-infused riot of a film. By not watching it, he hopes to keep it beckoning in his future. So he wanders (he thinks) into the streets, looking for a party but instead finding a vision of refugees, smoke, ruined buildings. 'Birthing angel of freeze-dried blooms / Seize the madness of this day' (Scene Six, p. 58) he cries out, and then language itself seems to break open:

> Deep slit of night murmur the tongue cut wide open by empires of no mercy in the pitch scarlet ride dank aching misery of history's pale light hold still the sky surrender the curling child splintered in the morn…
>
> (Scene Six, p. 59)

These words describe a rupture in time and space, and they also take the form of such a rupture, the sounds that are made by a 'tongue cut wide open.' It is the feeling of a vision of an angel, terrifying and passionate; and, as the vision lifts and he finds himself back in his room, he feels that he has been sailing, 'As if on some odd, enchanted ship / Made of film and light and darkness' (Scene Six, p. 59).

Where the budding artist is transported out of himself, a mirroring journey begins from the Jarman-figure's realization of his own mortality and the confines of the ship of his body. In the midst of trying to finish *The Last of England* – the film that will later transport the budding artist – comes the diagnosis that he is HIV-positive. Svich gives her Jarman foresight, his future 'stretched out like a liquid painting along the horizon' (Scene Seven, p. 63). More than the facts of the world to come, his vision mimics a camera, panning, focusing, cutting – dissolving the material world into fragments of feeling. Maybe he sees the budding artist, or someone like him, 'Brutalized, heart-ravaged, but still walking, / Still leaving trace upon the sand' (Scene Seven, p. 63). The artist's eyes fails him like a cracking lens – 'A river of arrows into my eyes' (Scene Seven, p. 65) – but the visions do not stop. His own angel of history visits him – Tilda Swinton, 'The tall woman with translucent skin,' who spins wildly in her wedding dress in *The Last of England*'s fiery final scene. What kind of angel is this? And what kind of history? Not only irrevocable, not just catastrophe, but also hope and transfiguration in the way that 'Time mirrors memory' (Scene Seven, p. 64). I think Svich suggests that it is not just that works of art will last through time, outliving their creators – but more than this, that they may grant visions that pierce, like arrows, the skin of history.

And one more conjunction, one more rift in time, which I was fortunate to experience firsthand. Earlier in his life, before going to art school and turning to film, Jarman completed his undergraduate studies at King's College London. This is where I was working in the autumn of 2014, when *JARMAN (all this maddening beauty)* was presented as part of the university's annual Arts and Humanities Festival. It was performed at King's by John Moletress of Washington DC-based performance ensemble force/collision. The idea for *JARMAN* arose from conversations between Moletress and Svich, and the piece was written for him. To watch Moletress perform was to watch an artist working at the very limits of his ability, for this is obviously a challenging text, switching tones and voices, and calling for mediated images that are open to the performer's interpretation. Moletress's version was punctuated by projected images created in collaboration with numerous DC-based performers, recalling the filmic language that Jarman used, but populating them with bodies that have come of age in a world after Jarman. How, then, to connect the two times? The text itself charts this effort:

> It feels as if a galaxy is between us.
> I start with the body,
> Its curves and lines.
>
> (Scene Nine, p. 72)

So Moletress, too, starts with the body – with beautiful, raging bodies on film, and also with his own body, here, in the room with us. Watching Moletress teeter gorgeously, precariously, in stiletto heels and a tattered tutu, in this place where Jarman once studied, and looking down the River Thames toward the warehouses where he would later live and work, it was as if, for a moment, the angel of history stopped fighting the storm and instead let its force propel him into this beautiful, maddening dance across time.

Performing *JARMAN (all this maddening beauty)*

John Moletress

Pottsgrove Senior High School
Pottstown, Pennsylvania
1993 September

The word of the day is
QUEERFAG

Popped out of the box without glitter and fanfare. A lick on the lips of your Joes and your Jims. I scurry through the glass doors, sun burns bright on parked cars and macadam. Into the swimming with sharks. Grapples for keys, brushes sweat off forehead, knuckles bear down on the steering wheel of my white Mustang, determined to leave the parking lot of Pottsgrove High as quickly as I came. Not even the refuge of the Choral Room, a frequent hideaway, could control the burning in my stomach. Not even hall passes discreetly forged on pink pads could passport my way out of the maze of maroon and white. Nor fucking my neighbor slash star quarterback of the football team for the past three years, my longest 'relationship' to date could in some, tiny little way provide some sense of belonging to the 'ordinary' teen cult. The key always sticks and the door jam is rancid. Flicks sweat off forehead. Reclines. Checks mirrors. Was that the quarterback with the Jims and Joes? Should I expect his phone call in 30? Put this shit in reverse and gas up the engine. Figures in rear view sharks making mountains on land.

Orientation

Art is violent. Art is queer. Art throws bolts into corporeal machinery, destroys and re-orientates. Art has the power to be transformative, unidentifiable, fluidly changing in time and space. A second gaze may betray the first. I feel this when I watch a Derek Jarman film. The work is tough, violent, penetrating, ever-evolving through states of beautiful destruction. His images are timeless, spatial constructions of liminality. As they rush across celluloid, the observer is faced with multiplicities of interpretation.

Derek Jarman was more than film. He was an avid painter, scenic designer, gardener, activist, and lover. *JARMAN (all this maddening beauty)* is a performative gesture inspired by Jarman. The production orientates itself to both present and past, gazing upon the icon through imagined territories and constructed spaces. The text explores the distant and not-so-distant Derek Jarman, making room for the possibility of a conversation across time.

When Caridad Svich and I were standing outside of the rehearsal room at New Dramatists in New York City in May 2013, we did not discuss crossing my own biography into the piece. Even though the ambiguous budding artist in JARMAN is performed as autobiography, it is not. I take in her text and imbibe it with imagination and wonder about the possibilities of parallels.

> No.
> This is something else,
> Something about violence itself,
> Violence against the body,
> The act of transgression against flesh and bone
> And how oddly beautiful it can seem –
>
> (Scene Two, p. 41)

I expose wounds for the material. The proximity to the work is no longer at a safe distance. This excites me. To connect deeply with the budding artist, I construct him from blood and bone, blurring the lines of truth and fiction. This was a key in finding Derek Jarman – the key in bringing him on stage. It is this intervention that allows Derek Jarman, both authentic and 'character,' to be conjured on stage as a phenomenological figure. He could come to the stage as a memory of the VHS tape of *Sebastiane* once played in my youth.

The performance begins with the body as a manifestation of the quality of that VHS tape, scratchy, shaky, and with poor tracking. Edited home movies from my childhood are projected on to the walls, interrupting notions that this temporal site is solely Derek Jarman's. The twine frame of an upside garden hangs over the space, anticipating its construction. Memories come in and out of focus, indicated by body and spatial aesthetics. This is a place where time and space are irregularly oriented. Two distant figures, a 'galaxy' away, meet:

> I light a candle.
> I roll out a long scroll of paper.
> I pick up my brushes and paints
> And begin to draw.
> The stillness of the city surrounds me.
> I see another light across the way.
> It feels as if a galaxy is between us.
> I start with the body,
> Its curves and lines.
> Look.
> […]
> Look at all the blooms.

Look at them all taking over the garden.
It's late summer.
I don't pretend that I am strong anymore
I am embracing fragility,
My fragility.

(Scene Nine, p. 73)

In *You Are Here: Personal Geographies and Other Maps of the Imagination,* edited by Katherine Harmon, Stephen S. Hall says that

> 'Orienteering' is such an odd but impressive word that it has always stuck with me, and in fact moves me to propose a related concept to describe a process somewhat like orienteering but more person, more historical, more associative, more metaphorical, perhaps more spiritual: 'orientating,' or crashing through the larger landscapes of memory and experience and knowledge, trying to get a fix on where we are in a multitude of landscape that together compose the grander scheme of things.

(Hall 2004: 15)

What Hall suggests is that geography not only physically orientates us to a particular place but also works upon our psyche and imagination – the psycho-geographic (Knabb 2005). We are drawn to places of experience, places that play upon our personal psychologies. Although I rarely visit the home of my upbringing, I have not forgotten the way, the sights, the markers that guide me there, and other memories associated with the journey. Through cornfields and on to the stone Colonial that protrudes out on to the 'T' of Orlando and Needhammer Roads, I close in on the distance from me to my memory house. Five houses from my childhood and my gaze cuts left to the rancher whose yard is littered with metal scraps and Christmas lights, the former home of the quarterback. Many moments of early sexuality and desire take possession of recollection.

What if we regard geography as also a place of institution, such as queer geography or celluloid geography? Queerness and celluloid contain within many maps of their histories and situations within a global landscape. Geographic identities play throughout *JARMAN*. My experiences with territories contained within are separated by time and space. My own experience of the material is separated by time and space. In 1996, I spent a semester in London studying performance abroad at Goldsmith's College and Laban. Although I took in every experience I could, the landscape did not bring me any closer to communion with Derek Jarman, in so much as he and his work are inextricably linked to England's politics, persistence and punk.

'We are turned towards thing. Such things make an impression upon us. We perceive them as things insofar as they are near to us, insofar as we share a residence with them' (Ahmed 2006: 27). How does the material of Derek Jarman impress upon so many who are unfamiliar? This question spins me a list of considerations. How can this be made into a performative inquiry? How can this inquiry get up on its feet and dance around the studio? At first, I position

Derek Jarman as outsider looking in on the performance. I place his 'appearances' or textual embodiments in spatial locations that I consider complicated or 'hot.'

The performance script for the first section:

> House lights fade. The house manager walks across the stage towards a silver bowl down stage right, plucks a flower from bowl, hangs on a strand of twine. Loud sound. Radio static. Text begins 'one: the story of a boy.' Body positioned in upstage right corner. Fluorescent lights situated along the edges of the space, pop on like a dream/fantasy/gallery. I wear – pop vintage t-shirt cut like a crop top, costume ruff, Fruit-of-the-Looms briefs, striped knee-high socks, pink high heels. I stand in a position with my forearms against the wall, head on hands. A position that says 'dejected.' I am private, yet observed. Sounds of my own recorded voice coupled with the scratchy, violent noise of static feedback underscore. The choreography mimics through suggestion the adjustment and tracking of a VHS tape. I thrust, fall, contort, mend, complicate the body through the space as the narrative plays in voiceover. I begin with this initial image of a young boy wearing his mother's heels for the first time, negotiating balance while moving about the tricky plush carpet. This act is one of danger and excitement, the possibility of being caught and yet also comes from a place of innocence. Derek Jarman suggests disturbance.

Watching a Jarman is dangerous, if you're young and figuring out your way. My experience of watching this film – this scratchy old VHS whose tracking at times would go out of place, doubling the images, and making them jump around – was indicative of the quality of danger I wanted to integrate into my own body movement. The costume heels are six inch stilettos, making sharp movements of the body and balance, dangerous. Additionally, I was working with physicalizing the idea of curiosity and the misshapen body. One limb wants to be pulled in this direction while another in a second direction, as the focus wants to be pulled in yet a third direction.

Caridad's territories intermingle with my own danger:

You will be NORMAL.

What does that even mean?
All I wanted to do was to kiss the boy's lips.
Caress his skin.

You will be NORMAL.

My mum never said that.
She never said 'be normal.'
I was a lucky child.
                    (Scene Three, p. 43)

> The football player... I remember. He moves in next door, 1989. We are 12. He was not yet the football player he would be, but his predisposed athletic body would turn him into the JOCK at the center of the requirements of masculinity. His father left one leg in Vietnam. Perhaps, he forgot it? His house is a rancher, except for a basement with misplaced and ill dumbbells, some filled with water and sand. His life enters the house, I enter the house, and he enters me. I remember his face. It was admirable. A MASC face disguised by a certain non-present maternal figure. He enters me when I enter his house, entering through the aluminum door that swings and makes noise...

Duplicitous in creative thinking mires the lines of fact and fiction. My truths bubble from the gut and spin around the dreaming of the text:

> The facts of this story may be imagined, the stuff of fiction –
> This is the story of a boy, after all,
> A boy who made pictures,
> And the story of a story of what's dreamt in time,
> Miles away, by someone else, and those here,
> Right here,
> Sometime later, believing in the myth of a story told for a night –
>
> (Scene Seven, p. 61)

Scene Six and the budding artist is thrown into the celluloid of *The Last of England* by a force of his making and yet not of his making. The barriers between past and present, media and liveness become fluid. Time and space collide to make room for the figure to be present in moment. Presence is as both corporeal and ephemeral. The figure is ephemeral insofar as the performance itself has a beginning, middle, and end. The corporeal nature of the figure is the transmission through my own body in performance. Dramaturgical research, studio processes, sketching and feedback take part to distill my performative intention into the life of Jarman.

Through the structure of Svich's text, a navigation of both memory and dreams, the act of arrival is always being renegotiated. The iconic figure can manifest only through the experiences of others.

> And the story of a story of what's dreamt in time,
> Miles away, by someone else…
>
> (Scene Seven, p. 61)

Svich's text is an imagined transmission of the world existing between fact and fiction. The proximity of my performance of the budding artist and the text is close; however, I am not this person. Memory can be illusive. Memory can betray us. What seemed to be one thing can be another thing entirely. Events blur together and our minds fill in the gaps.

Derek Jarman is a cypher. Through research, I have pieced together my own relationship between him and the work. The experience of the budding artist is meant to exist within universality. The specifics of the events leading up to self-discovery are not as important as a realization in time. The distance between fact and fiction is blurred because it is, after all, performance.

Berlin
October 2014

On tour performing *JARMAN (all this maddening beauty)*, I took a pit stop in Berlin to rediscover my proximal romance with it. I had not been since 1997. Call it youth, call it curiosity, call it a love for ambitious architecture and imagined spaces, my infatuation with Berlin runs deep. Endless seeing. Endless ways to get lost and caught up in the geography of steel cranes and buildings teetering on the edge between now and then. It is a world of violence, separation, fierce character, and ultimately, radical redemption. Berlin is the mother of liminality. She unrests her yarn upon the historical. Her geography is a cypher for puppeteers, scholars, and artists. Where one stop was taken, another was born. Berlin is the distance between birth and death. Within her heart, captivating is where sight is most relevant. Berlin was at a parlor and once told a joke that began, 'once upon a time in Austria' and nobody laughed.

When you say Jarman some think you said German. Jarman is German to a certain extent. Derek Jarman brings us to this place, the place where Svich takes imagination and weaves it through tapestries of temporal planes. Svich imagines a life for the budding artist at the heart of her play. Her words proclaim arrival for an unknown destination past food and fuel, space and time, past biography. Svich is a literary travel agent who digs deep, deep down into foreign territories armed with keyboard and carry-on, taking flights through wild dreams. Here the collision is par for the course. Svich and myself on a transatlantic flight.

Unless we've been to the Staatliche Museum in Berlin
And seen it up close.

(Scene Two, p. 40)

The words of the budding artist in *JARMAN (all this maddening beauty)* dare my inner artist to go out and play. At the center of the maze is the misunderstood minotaur named Sebastian – Sandro Botticelli's Sebastian to be exact. Memories weave through consciousness, only to emerge through the act of play. Svich tugs at the reigns of deer through childhood fascination, propelling the listener through imagistic landscapes.

I'm almost there.
Potsdamer Platz Station

I took the S-Bahn to the Potsdamer Platz and now walk a bit to the Staatliche Museen zu Berlin, pay the entrance fee, and enter the Gemäldergalerie. Gazing through corridors and ancient scenes of Christian heroics, cherubs cut against sky blue clouds and faces pallid and rose colored against varying spectrums of light; the agony and ecstasy of 500 years of European painting overwhelms. Botticelli's saint appears. Tethered to wood and immortalized with tempera on canvas, he hangs upon the wall, which hangs upon the structure of the entirety of the Gemäldegalerie. The saint is smaller than I had imagined. Fantastical imagination cannot be measured in metrics. He looks fragile, as if breath might blow him from his position, turning canvas to dust and retreating into memory. He is beautiful. The arrows enter him beautifully. Hedda Gabbler once said of death, 'do it beautifully' (Ibsen 1974).

Giovanni's Room, America's Oldest Gay Bookstore.
Philadelphia
September 1993

ENTER.

A bell on the door.

Is he looking at me? Is he wondering why I'm here? Is that pornographic? Do they sell pornography? This calendar looks awfully sexy. Should I be looking at this? I saw a film once. It went boy meets boy in a locker room, boy fondles boy, boy sort of kisses boy, boy pulls down boy's singlet, boy makes boy.
    Where the hell am I? Acid reflux. Want to look closer but what will they think? Checks around for other boys looking. Picks up book of dreams in 16-year-old hand; rings clip the pages to reveal Toms in a place called Finland. For which it stands, one nation under leather restraints. Breathe, said the vocal coach as he took me under the piano.

I'm arrive
I'm ah
I'm ahh
I'm ahhhhh
I'm arriving

This is where I meet Sebastiane for the first time.

He stands there oddly stuffed in the video racks between
Scenes of gay men playing hide the tongue
Scenes of forlorn lesbians
Camp queens
Sordid lives
ON SALE for $10.99 on VHS
Shit
I have 10 dollars.

It is not my knowledge of the film that makes me finger it from the stacks, but rather my imagination of the *highly attractive-ness of someone named Sebastiane.* SEBASTIANE. Who is Sebastiane? Esses so good on strawberry Chapstick lips smack the word honey and vinegar. Sebastiane must be from France. Pornography is from California. He is pain. Grasp hold steady. Stop shakes. Hold steady. Stop shakes. Heavy action making thin air into pie. I release the grip and place him back on the shelf facing outward in my direction. Staring. He whips me in colors of purple and flesh, notice the ribs protrude in high definition, stares at the sky, wonders why the pain. The smoke of Philadelphia becomes fog, as surroundings grow foreign. How do I get home? Where are Jim and Joe?

Fingers twitch. Look around. Rear view mirror clear. Tugging again on the VHS, I'm met with violent arrows darting from holes in the skin. Italian-looking, not Italian of Little Italy boy, stipple of hair upon the face, emanating aura of raptured pain. SEBASTIANE. The name sirens loud in my brain. Come. Please now thank you. Take the pigskin's place and give way with me. SEBASTIANE. Never a word fell off the tongue so sugar coated and sweet. He is pain, I can tell because I know. SEBASTIANE. Wherefore art Sebastiane? Where are you looking? Looking somewhere else? What do you see? Look at me. I'm here. I've arrived. SEBASTIANE. Sounds not like Robert, or Jim and Joe, or Bobby, Ted, and Sean. Sebastiane has a cock that doesn't look like mine. Mechanics are different but I've seen it before in Biblical art. My gaze gets lost in the imagery, drives deep down into parallax. Fog whooshes around like Dorothy on the farm, gains breath, and then begins to settle. Sebastiane is no ordinary boy.

Giovanni's taught me how to stare. So long are the days when the gaze of a young queer could bring about the arrows of words and violence. The printed map, which brought me to the bookstore, has now manifested itself as a performance text imagined by Svich.

> Only once his eyes show deep distress,
> Gazing in a painful nakedness;
> Then, as though ashamed of noticing,
> seem to let go with disdainfulness
> those destroyers of a lovely thing.

(Rilke 1957: 23)

I imagine digging deeper into the polarities between performing extreme intimacy and wild atmospheric states of space. I imagine states of intimacy playing themselves out through acts of complete presence and simplicity.

I think about the issue of finding myself within the work. This seems a broad idea, but hiding or being hidden is directly related to proximity. How do we uncover ourselves through our art? How do we orientate ourselves to the archive of work that has come before? How do we find our unique voice? Or, what do I have to contribute? In the process of attempting to be a particular 'something' that is unique, I often lose sight of the fact that all of the work comes from somewhere. It all stems from research or an idea that burns at the back of the brain. This 'thing' was planted there from a pre-existing experience wanting to be explored or examined. I think of 'newness' as a false concept. I do not work with new materials. Shapes are pre-existing insofar as materiality is molecules already in motion. Materials are flexible. I think of alchemy and the alchemical images at the heart of Derek Jarman's films. I approach Derek Jarman with a sense of re-arrangement.

I will engage the violent act of trust. Digging deeper and bearing down on the material, I will give myself permission to get lost. The making of art does not require an external

Global Positioning System. Rather, the GPS is internal. There is no separation between perceived boundaries of space and the body. To move freely and adapt becomes the nature of the process. There is no 'like' or 'dislike' in art, only metaphors.

As the work continues to be performed, *JARMAN* will continue to explore the extremes of proximity. When can the performance become more intimate, closing the lens to the equivalent of a pinpoint? When can the figure of Derek Jarman become even larger and more overwhelming, like the memory of self-discovery? How can extreme use of spatial relationship inform the proximity between Derek Jarman and myself? Distance is crucial to the process. It allows me the freedom to step away and find new patterns, new forms of expressing Svich's poetry.

References

Ahmed, Sara (2006), *Queer Phenomenology: Orientations, Objects, Others*, Durham: Duke University Press.

Hall, Stephen S. (2004), 'I, Mercator', in *You Are Here: Personal Geographies and Other Maps of the Imagination*, Katherine Harmon (ed.), New York: Princeton Architectural Press.

Ibsen, Henrik (1974), *Hedda Gabler*, Michael Leverson Meyer (trans.), London: Erye Metheun.

Knabb, Kenneth (ed.) (2005), *Situationist International*, Berkeley: Bureau of Public Secrets.

Rilke, Rainer Maria (1957), *Poems 1906–1926*, J.B. Leishman (trans.), Norfolk: New Directions.

Svich, Caridad (2014), *JARMAN (all this maddening beauty)*, unpublished second draft, September.

JARMAN (all this maddening beauty)

Caridad Svich

Figure 1: Performer and director John Moletress in *JARMAN (all this maddening beauty)*. Produced by force/collision © 2015 Deyanire Musa. All rights reserved.

This text for live performance is inspired by the life and work of British artist Derek Jarman (1942–1994).

All of the text is original. It is not taken from any of Jarman's writings.

This piece may be performed by one performer embodying the triptych of voices herein: the artist, the budding artist, the lover.

The role of the muse may be pre-recorded.

In staging, the work welcomes the use of video, projection design, sound-score, and choreographed movement.

Notes

// in the text indicates a slight shift/turn emotionally.

Italicized text that is not in parentheses is meant to be spoken.

Script History

The piece was written for the force/collision ensemble in Washington DC, directed by John Moletress (http://force-collision.org/jarman).

One: The story of a boy

This is the story of a boy.
This is the story of a boy who made pictures.
This is the story of that same boy when he was a man
And kept making pictures
And books and gardens too.

Beautiful gardens.

This is the story of a boy who loved his mum and his dad and his sister
And other boys too.
Lots of other boys.

You see, this boy liked other boys
Even though it was forbidden –
That is, the expression of his desire was against the law
In the country where he lived
Back in the day
When he was growing up.

They called his country England.
They still do.
But he knew
He knew it had become
A wreck of a country long ago.

And yet, and yet
He loved it.

Even though the empire was long, long gone.

You see, this boy liked to dare.
He spent his life daring.
All for love?

(A moment.)

This boy became an artist.

Some said he was strange.
Some said he was a genius.
Some said he was a kind of angel.

Queer angel.
Mad, defiant, raging…

Some don't even know who he is now.

Is that the way of all artists?

(A moment.)

This boy had a muse.
It was a woman – a tall woman with translucent skin.
She's famous now.
In some circles.
Well, in many circles, actually.

But when he met her, when he met her,
She was simply
Who she was.

And she gave him
Everything.
Everything of her.

She was light.
Still is.

(A moment.)

This is a story of a man who made pictures
And one day got sick,
Very sick
From a terrible plague that was going 'round –
A plague that seemed to affect
Other boys and men too.

A sad plague. Litany of dead.

Fuck death, he said.
Fuck irony.
Fuck the hurt inside me.

(Breath.)

This is a story of an artist who went blind
But even in his last days
Kept making
Pictures in his head.

Beautiful pictures.

Two: beauty and violence (part one)

(First view. Now. The budding artist from this time encounters the past.)

I was in the cinema.
Fucking art-house down college road.
My friend had said: you have to see this.
It's by this director. From back in the day. Some queer fellow.

He said it, like, it was a joke or something.
Not being mean. My friend's not like that.
It's just that we're all queer now.
Word doesn't mean the same thing as it did once back in the day.

Let's just say: doesn't have the same charge of transgression.

Remember transgression?

It was all over Art once.
Fucking buzzword.

Transgressive objects of desire.

                (Breath.)

I said, fuck films, man.
Didn't we spend thirty-six hours the other weekend
Watching French New Wave and the Italian neo-realists?
Just give me popcorn.

He was, like, don't you want to be an artist?
I was, like, I don't know.
I just want to make money.

My friend said: you have to see this. It's called *Sebastiane*.
Prof clued me into it. It's not even on the syllabus.
It's outta this world, man. Outta orbit.
You'll see.

//

Fucking art-house down under a pub off of college road.
Fucking tiny screen on a wall.

I was, like, if this is shite, I'm going to
I'm going to make him watch spaghetti westerns next weekend.

But then this film starts, real arty, real sexy,
Amazing light,
Like a painting.
And these men,
These incredibly beautiful men…
Radiant with their bodies –
Like Roman sculptures.

And there's nothing Camp about it. Y'know?
Not really.
Not quite in the way you'd expect of,
Well, a queer film from those days.
You know what I mean.

Nothing against Camp,
But it's not everything.

This film:
It's like I'm watching a painting from the Renaissance
Except it is 1976,
And the whole thing is in Latin,
The entire thing.
I think Holy fuck,
What the fuck is this?
Where the hell am I?

Heartbeatingwonder
Floatingdeliriousecstasy

And there's this boy,
This actor,
Young, black-hair,
He's Sebastiane
The saint,
And he has this face
Like an angel
No lying
No Camp

No irony
Amazing
Amazing
Strange ecstatic purity of it all.

Heartbeatingwonder
Floatingdelirious

And the arrows pierce his skin
Over and over
Like in the famous painting

You know the one:
Sandro Botticelli, 1474.
The famous painting we all reference
But have never really seen in person
Unless we've been to the Staatliche Museum in Berlin
And seen it up close.
St. Sebastian protected us all from the plague.

(Breath.)

The arrows pierce his skin
And it is awful,
Just awful,
So sad.

And yet somewhere
As I am crying
And thinking about the ugliness
Of persecution
And the crimes that have been committed in the name of God
I am getting turned on.

And it's not an S & M thing.
(Believe me, I'd know.)

No.
This is something else,
Something about violence itself,
Violence against the body,

The act of transgression against flesh and bone,
And how oddly beautiful it can seem –

Okay. Foucault and the aestheticization of violence in art and all that.
All the great philosophers.
Yes. They've taught us. Time and again.
I've sat in on the lectures,
Done my time in philosophy class.
But this is the first time
I've actually made the connection
In mind and body.
And well, I am a bit ashamed, to tell you the truth,
Not out of some kind of willful naiveté.
But rather because I'd like to think I'm, you know, ordinary.
I'm fucking middle class, for God's sake.

But the truth is,
When the arrows pierce his skin,
I'm mesmerized.

(A moment.)

When the movie's over,
I sit there in that crap art-house
With the noise of the pub above me
Bawling my eyes out
And I don't even know why.

But I think somewhere inside
Maybe I really do want to be an artist
Even if no one cares,
Even if everything I do is forgotten one day
In the grand charade of global enterprise.

(A moment.)

Some bloke flicks the lights.
I see a couple making out in the second row.

Did they even see the movie?

Yeh. They did.

I walk out of the cinema. It's pouring rain.
Fucking pissing down.
I don't even think to slip into the pub for a drink.

I'm still thinking of Sebastiane.
And this queer fellow I've never met
Who made this movie back in the day
With probably not even the fraction
Of what it cost to make *Avatar* or *The Lone Ranger*.

How'd he do it?

I think I owe my friend, like, a gift or something.

Should I call him? Text him?
Tell him that this was the day that changed my life?
Will he want to take the credit?

(Breath.)

I'm liquid blue.
Rain soaked straight through my jeans and blue T.

I don't want to call him right now.
I don't want to hear anyone's voice.
Not even a text.
I'm dreaming in Latin.

Pectus pectoris pulsus mirror Speculum mihi[1]

I'm painting in my mind. It's like an opera in my brain.

All this
All this
Cuz of a movie.

Three: beauty and violence (part two)

*(Second view: Then and Now.
The artist in memory subjective and subject to… after the film….)*

He stood there for hours.
My Sebastiane.

I replayed him in my mind.

*From fairest creatures we desire increase,
That thereby beauty's rose might never die,*[2]

This is beauty.
This is violence.

Love it.
We all love it.
Naked, glorious
Divine.

It was a movie.
But then, back then,
In that moment,
No…no…
It was more than that.

I was painting.
Every line,
Muscle,
Arrow cut through skin.

And then yes, yes:
Sebastiane and his lover in the water
In the stream,
Their bodies rolling and glistening
In the heat of the sun,
Their arses kissing the daylight
With abandon.

WE ARE LOVERS

Their bodies shouted.

WE ARE LOVERS.

No one could say anything.
Because
There they were – without shame –

It was a scandal. A glorious scandal.

But to me,
To me
It was church.

Even though I'm an atheist.

THIS IS MY CHURCH.

(A moment.)

What is art?
What is beauty?
How do we measure it?
What are the rules that govern art?
Who gets to say?
A friend of mine once said that Art was an excuse for a drink.
If you needed a drink, but found yourself making art instead,
Well then, perhaps you had stumbled onto something.

Another friend of mine used to say: Art is drink.
End of story.

Imagine discussing art like it mattered –

Does it anymore?
Aren't there more important things?

Crumbling cities
Toppled governments
Raging everything…

Yes
Yes
Yes

But Art lives in spite of…
I like to think.

We'd all like… wouldn't we?
Deep down?

Somewhere inside us
We like to think
All this raging creation
We call art
Must live.

Out of chaos and disorder
Out of the minds of those cast aside by…

Peevish schoolmasters
Beating students for bad behaviour

Beating me blue when I was nine
At boarding school

Riotous blue
Harsh blue
Numbing poison
Numbing me to all desire.

You will be normal, he said.

What does that even mean?
All I wanted to do was kiss the boy's lips. Caress his skin.

You will be NORMAL.

My mum never said that.
She never said 'be normal.'
I was a lucky child.

When I went back to bed
I couldn't even lie down properly.
He'd beat me so bad.

Numbed to all desire.

He should be ashamed.
A grown man – a schoolmaster – beating a child.
And he has the gall to say he believes in God.

Shame.

(*A moment.*)

Look at him: my Sebastiane.
Look at them all queuing up for hours to see what I've made.

Integrity, proportion, clarity.
Isn't that what St. Thomas Aquinas said?

Integritas, consonantia, claritas:
These are the qualities that define beauty in art.

I surrender to beauty.
I lift it up.

All Gloria in extasis to the heavenly cock.

This is my voice.
This is how I make things.
The camera is my eyes.

Claritas of self-revelation.

Do you see yourself in my Sebastiane?
Do you dare see yourself in this dream of youth?

Rock and blight,
Heat and water,
Sand against skin,
A mere cloth draped across his body.

Roll film.
Sweet dying England, you have no idea what I'm to make of you.

(*And after a while....*)

The projector hums.
The audience has walked away.

'All today's parties
Will leave without a trace.'

Someone sings in the alleyway
Getting the Velvet Underground all wrong.

Figure 2: Performer and director John Moletress in *JARMAN (all this maddening beauty)*. Produced by force/collision © 2015 Deyanire Musa. All rights reserved.

I look at the empty screen.
I still see him.
Still see Sebastiane.

When you beseech me, Sebastiane,
Will I answer you?
Or will your gaze haunt me for the rest of my life?

Pity the world, or else this glutton be,
To eat the world's due, by the grave and thee.[3]

Four: crap England or another word for jubilee

(The artist midst the maddening crowd… for love of country.)

Look.
It was clear.
If you were going to make something in this crap England,
You were just going to have to make it.
Nobody was going to sponsor you.
Unless you wanted to compromise.

It's not like the film and TV people
Were going to give you loads of money to make a picture
If they did, when they did, it came at a price.
Always does.

There may have been a queue to see the film,
And it may have run for months at that one cinema,
But someone else was making the money.
It's not like we were handed bloody receipts.

This may have been over-ground
But we were still under.
Not official, if you get my meaning.

Never official.

And even when we were
Sort of,
Later, much later,
New Queer Cinema and all that,
We still weren't.

It was all: 'Shove aside now
We don't have time for all this "personal cinema" bollocks
Maybe if you give us a rewrite?
Eh, darling? Something with a narrative through-line?'

I work with Shakespeare, Marlowe, Britten, and Wittgenstein.
If that doesn't show I can work with narrative,
Then…

Fuck narrative.
Fuck the rewrite.

I just want to make my movie
However, whenever I can.

If I sit and wait
And wait
And wait
And wait

What good's it?

No price on my dreaming.

No price on my dreaming.

We'll find the money where we find it.
Shoot without license.
Shoot on the street.
Make it up.

We got two hours
Come on. Let's get our friends together.
One side of the street and go.

Super 8 wonder.
Blow it up.
Make it fast
Hard
At the speed of dreams.

1600 cuts in six minutes.
Fuck it all to bits.

This is what I want to make NOW.
This is the England I see,

And will see again
When the last of England will befall us all
During Mrs. Thatcher's New Jerusalem:

(The following may be sung:)

'Kill your poor'

Chaos from within.
Kicking the street.

Steel toes in sockets.
Babies set alight.
Fire along the shoreline.
Ghosts of war –
No retreat, no surrender.

White noise. Angry guitars.
Wild-haired lads and lasses in studs and plaid
Raining a bloody rain on the reign of the Queen's silver jubilee.

Slit tongues
And a bleeding garden.

Cry, beloved dirt
The story of our birth.
Wreck the silver fork
Of dreaded obedience.

Grey battered skies
Against a shop window's gleam.
Fuel the battle cry
Of leaded deliverance.

Kill your poor, oh England
Dig their graves.
Blasted night of Furies
For the hell you'll pay.

Kill your poor, oh England
Sell their skins.
Wretched night of Furies
For the sins you'll sin.

Crown your lovely martyrs
With flaming thorns.
Seek perdition's glory
In Jubilee's scorn.

Adorn your greed
In misery's need.
Kill your poor, oh England
Damn their seed.

Five: Jubilation

(Later, much later, in Dungeness,
when the artist finds his lasting love,
we hear the lover's voice.... the first section of this may be sung.)

'The lover's song'

When I think of Derek,
When I think of this man I loved,
I think of angels.

When we lived in the garden
In the garden of this man I loved
I think of hope.

Out of shale, rock,
timber,
And poetry
We made a home

Out of touch, skin
Craving
And all
We made things whole.

I'd sing to him
In his last days
In the time we had together

Little songs of hope.

I'd sing to him
In his last days
Through the love we had together

Little songs of oak.

Through the trees
A smile
Through the threes
A stone

What will you give me, love?
I will give you a poem.

(spoken) And he'd take out his sketchbook
Or simply write in the air
Dazzling signs of witness
To some imagined creation.

(sung) Through the trees
A smile
Through the trees
A stone

What will you give me, love?
I will make you a home

(Breath. The following may be spoken.)

In the days of sadness
That followed the days of jubilation
I wondered why he still loved England.
Because it's mine, he'd say.

Beauty. Must make beauty.
Those bastards can kiss my arse
If they think they're going to poison this country without a fight.

Another smile.
And a burst of color filled his drawing –
A wondrous sky.

Six: blasted earth and the sea of all dreams (part one)

(The budding artist yearns for the art object.)

I hold the DVD in my hand.
On the cover, the despairing face of a tall woman with translucent skin
Is framed against a radioactive sky.
She wears a wedding dress
That she will soon tear
In furious strokes
With an enormous pair of scissors.

I haven't seen the movie yet,
But my friend,
The same friend who encouraged me to go to the art-house that time,
Has told me about it.

I'm telling you, man, Wait til you see it. Just wait.

//

I hold the DVD in my hand like an emblem.
I am afraid to open it.
The image on the cover alone sends shivers down my spine.

Look, I'm not a weakling. I go to slasher flicks, right?
I've seen horror films. But most of them don't mean anything to me.
It's just popcorn.

But this is different.
Because I've already seen
Jubilee, The Tempest, The Angelic Conversation, and *Caravaggio*.
I'm making my way through all of Derek's films –
The ones I can get my hands on, at least.
I come to each one now with a set of expectations.

Dazzle me. Disorient me. Teach me.
Open me up to the world and all of its possibilities
Savage me to art.

And this one, this one, well…
I know what I'm in for.
I know this ride will be cruel, harsh and devastating.
My friend told me.

And he doesn't lie.
Not about movies, anyway.

(Breath.)

I think somehow if I hold the object in my hand
I can dream a little longer.
I can be safe
And dream my own dreams of blasted innocence
And not Derek's.

We are on familiar terms now.
This artist, whom I have never met,
And who passed away in the late 20th century,
Has become a kind of friend.
My sweet, funny, nervy, impulsive, ill-tempered, well-tempered friend.

(A moment.)

I stare at the cover for days.
I refuse to insert the disc.
I won't even stream the damn thing off of a rogue website.

It is perverse of me.
My friend texts: Have you seen *The Last of England* yet?

I don't answer.
Hours go by.

I pretend to do work.
I do laundry.
I lie on the bed and masturbate.
Anything
Anything
To not open the cover.

My friend texts me again. He is concerned.

I don't answer.
I won't answer.
I will see it in my own time.

Let me dream a little longer.
Let me imagine
What it's like.

It is perverse of me.

I want to wear that wedding dress.
I want to live in that still image.
Place me in the frame.

The DVD beckons.

I put it face down on the shelf.

It still beckons.

Perverse joke.

I slip it in between my hard copy of T. S. Eliot's 'The Waste Land'
A print-out of the Old English poem 'The Wanderer'
And George R. R. Martin's *Game of Thrones*.

Showing off? Or am I just another esoteric college kid?
Maybe a bit of both.

Well, that's that.
The DVD is on the shelf.
It is tucked away safely.
No need to look at it now.
If it will be, it will be on another day.

//

I walk out of the flat, keys in hand
Determined to have a good time.
The promise of sex, drink and
Burning like a Roman candle across the night fills me.

I walk a good mile.
The streets rain coal.
The clouds are black and cold.
The earth spits fumes.

I walk as if in shadow
Alone.

Always the one alone longs for mercy.

Not a soul anywhere.
And the ones that are,
The ones glimpsed,
Seem wrecked to oblivion.
I keep walking.
I will have a good time.
I will do whatever to seek it out.

There's a crowd. In the distance.
I walk toward them.

They are skin and bone.
Some are crying.
Some are barely able to stand.
They have been traveling for centuries.

Refugees, they say.
We are refugees.

Sorrow bound in wretched exile.

Smoke rises from the streets.
Thick raging smoke.
I can barely breathe.

I look toward what seems like light,
True light.

Is there a party over there?
Is someone having a good time?

Are you?
Perhaps? In your own way?

Good.
Good.
Then we are together in this, you and I.

Let's check out the party.
Let's escape the masses of refugees.
Let's have a fucking good time.

And over there, over there, the ruined buildings are the works of giants.

I feel emboldened by the nearness of the impossible extreme.

We will all have a fucking good time,
And we will tell our so-called sons and daughters one day that
We were kings and queens.

//

I follow the pulse of sound – the looming party.
It is going to be a brilliant night.

I approach the light.
The hollowed eyes of masked militia stare at me.

What happened?
Thought this was a…
What in bloody hell…?

I am shaking.
I start to cry.
I shout words in a language that isn't mine.

(This may be sung.)

Cradlesong for no cradle
Birthing angel of freeze-dried blooms
Seize the madness of this day
Bone-remembered to the last.

(And then…)

I don't know where I am.
The road gives way.
Tremor and…

(And then… a montage of word/image…)

Cascade of nations guard loose self-sweet desires swollen black corridors flares and gunshots hold the tongue unnatural hold soon the body feathers the body grace at six and hundred six and ten thousand litany of the dead static resurrection of a broken land

Here, here, there and wherefore the sullen cry of the sodden crows dart bout the lingering watch of night strangled in a heap begging succor at Sycorax's breast born of another feral child of no man woman's son discarded angel of the runt cunt

Doom the boy to war past stories held in the cheek of a father witness to war's disgust mangled instinct and the desperate curl of leaves upon the desk where we once held hands like friends father and son brothers of the same country left in ruin while animals bathe their young

Deep slit of night murmur the tongue cut wide open by empires of no mercy in the pitch scarlet ride dank aching misery of history's pale light hold still the sky surrender the curling child splintered in the morn –

This here see I in tomorrow's fire left burning by revelers' delight against all shores in a dark picture house slapped by heaven's milk.

(And then, a stillness... for a long time.)

When I look around
I have somehow made it back to my flat
Despite the cold grey waves against my back.
Somehow,
Some other,
I am here.

And the DVD cover is there, off the shelf, opened.

The tall woman with translucent skin
Is holding me by the hand.

The wedding dress
She once wore
Is on the floor
Which has now become a sea.

We are both sailing
As if on some odd, enchanted ship
Made of film and light and darkness.

I think: This is the last,
The last of England.

Figure 3: Performer and director John Moletress in *JARMAN (all this maddening beauty)*. Produced by force/collision © 2015 Deyanire Musa. All rights reserved.

She turns and looks at me.
She whispers.
Yes.

Seven: blasted earth and the sea of all dreams (part two)

(The artist intimates his own mortality.)

It is four A.M. on a Sunday.
We had been filming all night.
The last of the Last of England
Was not yet upon us.

I was chest-deep in home movies
Made by my father years ago –
My father, the RAF pilot,
My once negative mirror to whom I am starting to feel closer,
Because the England he fought for in the Second World War is being lost.
We both see it.
These bits, these pieces of film, may be all that's left of the glow-worms.

That's us. We're the glow-worms.
See?

We are the ones slowly vanishing.
And in our stead will be this whole other species:
Devoid of any kind of glow at all.
Because it will all be about the right kind of cheese and shopping.

//

I am sorting out how I am going to collage
The footage that we have already shot
With what my father had given me.
I am furiously sketching at the same time,
Image after image,
Trying to figure out how it is all
Going to come together.
This picture is being made on the fly.
On the wings of angels, some say.

Should we film near the cliffs tomorrow?
The caves?
What will the light be like?

Like most filmmakers, I am attracted to twilight.
The perfect hour.

The time when something dies and something else is born.
Rebirth and tragedy. We're all in the same soup.
But, unlike other filmmakers, I am not married to twilight.
Sometimes you shoot when you have to shoot.
The magic and science comes later.

What I know is that this film has to be finished.
I can't spend years waiting, like I did with *Caravaggio*.
Stuck in some rewrite and funding hell,
Spinning my wheels.
And for what?

It was received well,
But I lost seven years of my life,
Seven years
Chasing that gorgeous, murderous monster.
I won't do that again. I can't.

(Breath.)

It is four A.M. on a Sunday
And I have just learned I am HIV-Positive.
December 22, 1986.

The facts in this story may be imagined, the stuff of fiction –
This is the story of a boy, after all,
A boy who made pictures,
And the story of a story of what's dreamt in time,
Miles away, by someone else, and those here,
Right here,
Sometime later, believing in the myth of a story told for a night –

But the date, this date is not:
December 22, 1986.
It is recorded on all timelines.

Here's your diagnosis, sir.
What will you do now?
Happy Christmas?

Well, there are drugs. And potent cocktails.
And some work. Really well to keep the virus at bay.

But I know, somehow I know, that I don't have much time.
Chestnuts roasting on no fire.
Bollocks to holidays.
This virus will work its way through me
Until I am fossil, flint, stone, shell.

I'm not one for doom.
I've always been rather optimistic about things.
I had a happy childhood,
Except for boarding school,
And even then, I found a way.

But here…looking out the window…
Out onto the sea
Where we will film
The scene with the wedding dress tomorrow,
The one that will grace DVD covers one day
And be the stuff of dreams of young artists
Who won't even know who I am,
And what this England was like –

All they might remember is loud noise, tartans, studs,
The iron will of the Iron Lady,
And later, after my time, the well-combed hypocrisy of Blair's Cool Britannia
And the blinkered rise of Cameron's austerity –

I know I am not long for this life,
Despite my love of and longing for it.

Premonition?
Or maybe just the knowledge that I may not fight this fight
The way others may like.

I'll fight it my own way.
Like everything else I've done.

I will likely be criticized for
Being open about my HIV-Positive status in the press
At a time when hardly any public figure in England even admitted to being gay,
And then, for not wanting to sustain myself over the coming years
On ever evolving, escalating combinations of powerful drug cocktails.

That bastard would have been alive today if he'd taken this, that and the other,
Some lad will say, anger swelling up in his voice.

Who knows how death will work,
How it will work on one's body?

No one, no one has the right to judge.

This is my story.
I'll live it how I choose.

So: To work, to doing, to stirring things up.
Fuck all.

Happy, happy Christmas.

And if this is my last movie,
Then it will be, as it is,
The fact of my life.

> *(Breath. And then, as if through glass, through water, the artist sees this moment and his future moment(s).)*

It's four A.M. on a Sunday.
I look out across the water:
I see my future stretched out like a liquid painting along the horizon.

This is what I see.

Flares in the sky.
Crimson threads against low restless clouds.

Along the shore?
Bones: remnants of humanity that survive millennia.
Flesh so mortal, so easily corrupted
Have surrendered their last goodbye.

I train my eyes
On a figure,
Brutalized, heart-ravaged, but still walking,
Still leaving trace upon the sand.

Focus, focus.

The figure has survived everything.
Every bloom, every ounce of decay,
Every touch rendered wanton.

Closer now.

Rock-stubbed vicious eyes plead peace
Before it is all over,
And we will be all over
In the fiery gloom.

And wide.

The heavens do not answer.
The heavens do not sigh.
There is a stillness across the land,
A stillness made of sound,
And heavy tears
And the skeletons of the citizens of the world.

Zoom in.

Glassy glimmer of light
Tricks desire into belief.
A potent anesthesia for coming devastation.

Cut to:

The believing figure lets out a howl
Made of gasoline.
The waters rise.
Nature charms youth.
Invincible ruin is
Invisible to ruin, the gulls cry.

And wider still.

Illness begets days of love
And restless creation.
Afflicted organs black out.
Time mirrors memory.
The soul becomes burdened with lies.

Which truth is my truth?
Which dream is truly mine?

Caravaggio's? Shakespeare's? Marlowe's? Sebastiane's?

Cut to:

Dusty daylight bears down.
A world of doing still left to do.
Acute pain hinders fingers from opening.
All fists now.
Curled ache.
The paint spills, spatters.
Ataxia.

The lens blurs.
No control. No finesse.

Fuck death.
Fuck irony.
Fuck the hurt inside me.
Fucking cunt, do your job.

Steady steady.

The lens cracks.
Iris shards on the wood floor.

Isn't this fun?
Isn't this a riot?

A river of arrows into my eyes.

And hold.

Retina detaches.
Muscles lose memory.
I am blind.

                        (Silence.)

The tall woman with translucent skin,
The tall woman, my muse,
Cleanses my feet.

'Wash the days of days away in the stirring wake of humanity.'

A song for no one sung beautifully
Against the shadow of the nuclear power station behind us.

An opera in my brain.

The tall woman with translucent skin kisses my feet.

How very Pieta.
I always wanted to live during the Renaissance.

We both laugh.
We can do that with each other.
We can mock and play and make bloody mischief.

We share confidences, as if we were a couple of adolescents skipping school.

We remember when we first met:
She opened the door
I trained my lens on her
And never stopped.

Don't stop.

We were wasted
High on everything
All beauty, all possibility within our reach.

I will go wherever you take me.

The light sparkled in her eyes.
Flecks of gold.

I swim in her pale radiance.
Until we are both asleep
Exhausted from the exhaustion of being close
And keeping the foul stink of death at bay
A tad longer.

My feet twitch.
Shiver.
An embrace.

Steady, steady.

Retina dissolves into…
Gelatinous substance in my palms.
Tears flow from unknown sockets.

And hold.

Just you and me and you
And the shadow of the sun.

We will remember laughing for hours.

My lover, the lover I will meet a year from now,
Will wrap us both in his arms,
And sing us his little song of hope.

For a while
We will be at peace
Like good soldiers.

Like the soldier my father was all those years ago.

And my mum will wave from the memory garden
The way she always waved,
With a tender smile
And a loving heart.

My sis will watch over me, the way she always does,
With appreciative bemusement
At the maddening beauties of my art.

All this maddening beauty, she'll say,
As she runs her hands over the silver tins of film,
And the rows of books, and the stacks of sketches and paintings,
And she'll say it with a bit of wonder.
All this maddening beauty, we will echo,
Letting the echo linger in the air
As we tremble a little
At the lusciousness of all that we imagine:

(Montage of word/image.)

Tall feathers, high collars, silver star shadows, billowing skirts, tight corsets, the length of corridors long and endless, caverned spaces against pools of black, as Bacchus flowers canopies of text that spool out in inky blooms across the floor,

Walls rendered in ivory streaked with stains of blood and piss and semen, sky blue wigs piled atop pale faces waiting for their fates to be decided, sailors jacking off to portraits of Cupid, lustrous wash of sepia as the road sparkles like tea poured in old kettles during winter while we wash our faces in the rivers and streams of our desires made pain by flesh,

Carrion crows fuck the heavens, their beaks pecking at the clouds, a shower of black feathers upon the humid earth as jets scream overhead promising mercy to no one, the whole globe shudders at the sound of the barking moon, while boys and girls play ashes, ashes, all fall down in their mother's garden, oblivious to all that surrounds them,

Lanterns line the docks where ships set sail at break of dawn, a constellation of cum along the boardwalk, crystal fairies cast their spells upon lonely mortals, plucking carnations for luck along the way while the swift song of ancient voices kneads the skin along the shoulder of the curved sky,

Heavens cry feasts of battle with a mere touch, I sink into your down and surrender what war is left in me, too many days in search of you, across the bitten night of your vein-less hunger, promises made in thick of night turned cold in the wake of bitter thunder, this spoon our spoon, the cock's crow cries, as we lay waste to our passions, rivers of you, thirteen ships strong, caress my slumber,

If echo be the echo found of looking through the looking glass, the looking eye will look some more for sweet, forgiving serenity.

(Stillness. And then…)

I will dream of sleep
And no sleep
And furious grass winding its way through the garden –
There, there tucked in between the roses and delphinium
Will be a lamb lying next to a crocodile.
They are feasting on each other.
Their wounds are open to the world.

Hurry time. Glow in the landscape of this design.
Glow, glow all my glittering glow-worms.
Gorge on the gaping wounds alight to the moon.

I'll wake with a start,
Except this time, there is no sun,

Only the blue black pitch of nothingness before my eyes,
Burning through my eyelids to the back of my brain,
As I reach for my lover's arms
And wait

For the rest of days.

//

Distant rumor of another plague.
Where's Sebastiane now to protect me?

(A moment.)

And when it is finished,
When I am,
When it was all
Finished,
We said yes,
This is the last of England,
And the sky turned serenely blue.

1987. The picture is released.

In seven years' time I will be dead.

Eight: every time we say

(The lover dreams of his lover.)

This was his last portrait,
The one here in the National Portrait Gallery.
It's called *The Seer*.
He wanted to sit for it.
He was chasing time.

Or perhaps it was the other way around.

In any case, this was the last official face
He gave the world.

Sometimes someone will stop me
Here
Right here in the gallery
And ask me about him.
It's usually some lad,
Fresh out of art or film school,
Or just someone wandering through their life,
Besotted with his films.

I just saw *Edward II,* he'll say.
'It's fucking intense. So ahead of its time.'

They usually don't know who I am.
I don't take the time to explain.
We lived a public life
Insofar as some things,
But most of the time, we were quite private, actually.

I was his lover, partner, mate, husband, confidante,
Fellow dreamer, and care-giver. I was his breath, his life.
We met a year after *The Last of England*.
We were both chasing time.

The lad looks at me.

Well, I respond,
I think *Edward II* is very much of its time, to be honest.

The young man is a bit bemused.
His eyes glimmer with the unmistakable ardor of prayer.
It's clear he has no idea what England was like then.
He probably has no idea what the world's like at all,
Despite everything at his fingertips.

The fight for our rights was fucking hell.
The Iron Lady and her crowd did not make things easy.
We fought teeth and smiles for every bit of LGBT recognition.
We're still fighting.

The conversation, if it continues,
Might then turn to matters of art and beauty.
But usually, these glowing young things
Just want to revel in the adoration of the artist who died relatively young,
Raging, raging out of time.

See beyond that.
Would you?

//

Look.
Look at him.
Look at that face.
He was still making mischief.
Even then.

(The following may be sung.)

'Passion song (lullaby)'

Live long passion
Live long the days
Red moon shines upon a sea
Of antiquity

Today we sing a song of horizons
While fireflies dance
And souls grant us grace.

Nine: aperture (a shared dream)

(The budding artist finds courage while the artist sees the world.)

Everything is dark.
It is nine o' clock in the evening
And the whole city's shut down.

My friend said this would happen.
He can predict things.
Or at least that's what I have come to believe,
After his prodding me to dive into Derek's work.

I have started to make digital films.
Little things. But I think something may come of it.
And I have started to paint, too.

See, man? I knew you were an artist (my friend says).

I don't know.
I'm just playing.
But for now, for now, it feels right.

//

I light a candle.
I roll out a long scroll of paper.
I pick up my brushes and paints
And begin to draw.

The stillness of the city surrounds me.

I see another light across the way.
It feels as if a galaxy is between us.
I start with the body,
Its curves and lines.

(The artist in his time speaks….)

> Look.
> Look at the blooms.
> Look at them all taking over the garden.

> It's late summer.
> I don't pretend I am strong anymore
> I am embracing fragility,
> My fragility.
>
> Look, she exclaims
> And I feel the warmth in her voice
> And imagine her smile
> The smile I cannot see anymore
>
> Because now
> There are only faint blurs
> Shots of grey
> And traces, on occasion,
> Of blue.

(And the budding artist in his time says….)

Blue.
Iridescent like the tattered sequins on that shirt
One of my friends left behind from that party that one time.
What are you doing with that fucking shirt?
Souvenir.

(The painting begins to materialize.)

Blue morning comes
While I wait for you
Even though I know you are gone.

> Blue-grey-black.
> A voice calls to me.

Derek?

> Everything fades
> Like the iris closing

Derek?

> Breath.
> Breath.

The garden sings a brutal song of blooms.
Listen.

(And perhaps we hear the garden's song for a moment or see the ocean waves crashing against the rocks beyond the garden. The drawing the budding artist makes expands – a digital garden?)

> Faces, eyes, cocks, thighs
> Faces, eyes, cocks, thighs
> Faces, eyes…

(And then…)

Arrow through skin.
Glimpse of Sebastian.

*(Do we see a glimpse? In Memory?
Beautiful naked Saint Sebastian pierced through with arrows?)*

> Faces, eyes,
> A trickle of blood…

Derek?

> And then a bird
> A robin flies over
> A lost robin looking for food?

> Come.
> Come to my garden, little robin.
> You are welcome here.
> Everyone is welcome in my garden.

The robin rests.
A slight breeze.

> Today is Tuesday.
> Yes. I remember now.
> I will be alive another five days.

Is that all the time you have left?

> In five days' time all of me
> Will be like the end of 'Stormy Weather.'

(And perhaps we hear a fragment of an old recording of 'Stormy Weather' for a brief moment.)

He takes his hand in mine.
We let the breeze touch our skin.

                                              Is it a red breeze?
                                       Shall we play that game?

                                                 Everything in life
                                                      Has a color.

                              I've a color palette for the whole world.

Let's call it a red breeze.
For now.
Soon it will be blue.

                                      (Time passes.)

                                          The cool labyrinth of night
                                                    Comes upon us.

I yield to flower
Petal
Stem
The iris of the iris…

                                                         Fade in.

                          I see myself walking along a corridor
                                             At school
                                         Long, long ago
                                 When I was a queer child,
                               The queerest child of them all.
                                     And I didn't know
                                 What queer really meant
                           And what it would come to mean
                                       Later, much later
                 When I was older and a new world had begun.

I remember drawing a picture at school
And the other children being scared of what I'd drawn.

Your child's imagination is over-developed, teacher told my mum.
He'd do well to curb it.

Mum nodded at the teacher's remarks
But she did not heed them
Mum knew I was made for this garden
Made to bloom.

Sweet as an English rose.

Late summer
And I am rocking out to an old tune

Loud hard screaming bollocks.
Scream a song of Jubilee. Bugger the world.

Is it quaint now to sing like this?
To miss smashing roaring punk?

I'll always miss it.
I'll always sing of you.

Discordant angel, come to me.

(A moment.)

And we see everything about everything that there is in the world.
We see it with our hands touch skin.
Our fingers dance the sky.

Roll film.

Let's begin.

Figure 4: Performer and director John Moletress in *JARMAN (all this maddening beauty)*. Produced by force/collision © 2015 Deyanire Musa. All rights reserved.

Ten: ardor (hidden track)

The tall woman with translucent skin appears.
She wears an exquisite dress.
She looks at him, as he looks at her from behind the camera.

(The muse on film. A rehearsal.)

Look where?

To the right?

Like this?

(SFX: Indistinguishable words from the artist heard in reply. Perhaps this is just a sound like waves or a held note on strings.)

How 'bout like this?

(SFX: indistinguishable words from the artist heard in reply. The muse laughs.)

You're making me laugh.
I'm trying to be serious here.
This is high drama.

(SFX: indistinguishable words from the artist heard in reply.)

Okay
Control.
Keep in frame.
And then when the…

Lift my arms.
Right.

(SFX: indistinguishable words from the artist heard in reply.)

What?

(SFX: indistinguishable words from the artist heard in reply. The muse laughs.)

Yes. Like we always say:

Fuck all.

FUCK ALL.

> *(She lifts her arms toward the heavens. It is a perfect, soaring image.*
> *Freeze.*
> *The image is magnified for a moment,*
> *And then is gone.)*

End of play

Notes

1. 'Heart beating wonder, mirror me.'
2. William Shakespeare, Sonnet I: line 2.
3. William Shakespeare, Sonnet I: line 14.

Laying Siege to *Carthage*

Pedro de Senna

Approaching a text as complex and poetic as Caridad Svich's *Carthage/Cartagena* is like laying siege to a city. One needs to be patient, to bide time. Encircle it. *Carthage/Cartagena* cannot be taken with a frontal attack – any attempt to tackle it head-on would surely fail. The text cannot be flanked either: it will not be caught by surprise. My advice to you, kind reader, is to live with it. Be around it. In time, it may open its doors, yield its secrets, let you in.

If I make use of language that sounds bellicose, this is not to imply any kind of antagonism toward the text. The martial vocabulary comes from the history of Carthage itself, 'Ancient land,' a city with many lives across time and space, reincarnations in different eras and continents: the famous Phoenician colony (now in Tunisia), which Roman troops besieged for two years before finally destroying it; but also Sudan, Spain, Canada, Colombia, Chile, Costa Rica, and multiple locations in the United States.

> Much war in this Carthage,
> In this Cartagenas,
> So much seen
> Felt
> In air
>
> (Canto One, p. 104)

There is of course one crucial difference: while these cities of the world are made of houses, streets, temples, and squares, Caridad Svich's Carthage is a city built with and peopled by words, echoes, memories, and dreams. The text as landscape. A landscape that needs to be taken in, not taken over; reconstructed, not destroyed. Yet, *Carthago delenda est*. Carthage must fall, and rise again, in our imaginations, on our stages. And yet again, like Hasdrubal's Punic stronghold, once penetrated, it needs to be taken house by house, line by line (of continuous absence). With every new line, a new struggle.

Eric Mayer-García describes the text as

> a series of multi-lingual letter-song-poems connected by themes of displacement, exile, and human trafficking. [It] dramatizes moments of 'desterrar', or being ripped away from homeland and finding oneself in a foreign land. The piece stages the violent origins of diaspora […].
>
> (Mayer-García 2014)

It is a text that might well be called 'postdramatic,' if for a dramaturg like me the expression did not seem oxymoronic. And so I would rather call it a 'landscape,' appropriating a term Elinor Fuchs proposes in *The Death of Character*. Writing about the work of Suzan-Lori Parks (*The Death of the Last Black Man in the Whole Entire World*), Fuchs suggests that 'The landscape effect of the play arises not so much from the playwright's use of natural imagery, but from the open, spatial form of the piece, written in visual "panels" […]' (Fuchs 1996: 104). However, it is not that the oppositional nature of drama has disappeared, as Fuchs suggests; but (at least in the case of *Carthage*) that the prevalence of imagery, the arrangement of the words on the page itself, camouflages it, as it were. The landscape needs to be taken in carefully, attentively, before you see the figures emerging from the background.

Carthage/Cartagena is a play written in verse and described by the author as 'ten cantos and a prayer for performance.' The text has no ascribed characters. It is a *Carta Ajena*, a letter from afar, from alien voices in English and Spanish, speaking (or perhaps singing, chanting, wailing) of dislocation, human trafficking, and war. It can be staged as a solo piece or as a piece for a chorus; or anything in-between. The play has been deemed unstageable.

Well, not quite. Here, the notion proposed by Patrice Pavis (1992), that staging is creating contexts in which the words of the text can be understood, can be very useful – even if this understanding is perhaps more phenomenological than semiotic. From the mass of words, patterns as well as characters and narratives start to appear. From the poetry and structure, something beyond the words themselves starts to manifest. Staging *Carta Ajena* has to be about this: allowing for this something to come to surface. Something that may be defined by the play's subtitle:

When I looked up, I looked for something (call it hope)

Hope that you will be able to find a stage language that might reflect and do justice to the written language of the page. Hope of writing this alien letter with our bodies. So when Svich – having seen SignDance Collective perform *The Other Side of the Coin*, a piece based on the *Ferias* series of poems by Federico García Lorca– decided to offer the text as a challenge to the company, she was aware that SignDance's trademark style fit hand-in-glove with her play.[1] Svich at the time praised the company's ability to 'create a genuine, unique theatrical world that lingers long in the mind after the performance is over' (Svich 2013). SignDance Theatre is a form of dance-theatre that has Sign Language as its choreographic basis and structuring dramaturgical/gestural device. The poetic language of the text is adapted to choreographic form in this way. Writing of the appreciation of dance-theatre, Babbage refers to a talk given by Patrick Flanery in 2008 where he discusses ballet audiences of adapted novels: 'anticipating subtraction of the verbal dimension, audiences of dance-theatre will expect a production that assumes a distinctively new shape' (Babbage 2009: 14). Dance-theatre therefore embraces that subtraction, that gap. In SignDance Collective's work, adaptations and translations from English and Spanish to Sign Language(s) to physical theatre and choreography seep through the interstices of the text, replacing, reshaping, reforming. One may argue that this is not strictly staging the text, but adapting it. Margarita Laera, however, suggests that 'the mechanisms of adaptation and those of theatricality have something fundamental in common' (Laera 2014: 3). So, to a certain extent, staging *Carthage* must be about the creation of aesthetic-linguistic contexts in which experience and meaning (the old phenomenological/semiotic divide) meld into one. SignDance Theatre does precisely that, reintegrating a verbal dimension, often embedded in the choreography. What we see, however, are only traces of words, phantom limbs.

To borrow Jo Machon's (2011) term, SignDance Theatre is a form where a '(syn) aesthetic' appreciation occurs, where the somatic and the semantic overlap. Again, writing about the landscape stage (as a corollary to the landscape text), Fuchs says 'I don't suggest that the dancer and the dance have melted into each other in this theatre, far from it. We experience distance, but without alienation, and on the other hand involvement, without identification. What then holds our attention?' (Fuchs 1996: 106). The answer, eminently performative, is given by Caridad Svich herself: 'we are still, in the end, in the theatre, left with the most dangerous, radical subject of all: the human being framed in space and light, governed by time' (Svich 2002: 19). The dialogue between Fuchs and Svich is productive in shaping an understanding of SignDance's work in general, and of *Carthage* in particular. Indeed, Svich argues that 'Theatre is about time. […] Meter, tempo, rhythm and silence are all elements of theatrical constructions of text and space' (Svich 2003: 3). Fuchs suggests that '[t]he common thingness of landscapes and plays erased any sense of contradiction between nature and culture, stationary figures and human figures, or visual phenomena and language' (Fuchs 1996: 94). The city built with words comes to life in the performers' bodies; its inhabitants are born out of their actions. Svich has proposed that 'the body in space is the cultural sign that is constantly being deciphered in performance' (Svich 2003: 11). This is particularly true of SignDance Theatre, when the deciphering of the body as it moves in space may or may not be informed by linguistic competence in Sign Languages, just as Anglophone readers and audiences may not fully understand the Spanish words contained in this sphinx-like text.

Mayer-García, commenting on the version of *Carthage* presented by SignDance Collective at the *NoPassport Conference* in 2014, stated that the performance

> speak[s] from the borderlands of the real, a space beyond representation and language, encircling the edges of trauma. The text of *Carthage/Cartagena* draws on multiple languages, English, Spanish, Italian, BSL, and ASL as a strategy to approach this 'unspeakable' space of trauma through the disconnected space between languages, and the gap between meanings lost in translation.[2]
>
> (Mayer-García 2014)

Perhaps one may speak of the trauma of staging (I will return to the notion of trauma later), and the gaps that, by definition, it leaves – and of the pleasure inherent in perceiving, filling, or simply accepting those gaps. Decipher me this. Indeed, *Carthage* is constantly playing with the enigma of language. Take, for example, this passage from Canto Three:

Wire cuts into my skin.
I want to scream
But I don't
I will not give them my voice

Nunca les dare mi voz

They do not look at me
They do not see me
I am garbage to them

Basura

But trade nonetheless

In the container
There are others
Tied, too
Silent, too
Some are crying

Como noche sin fin

(Canto Three, pp. 109–10)

Much of the pleasure of the text (as Barthes might have referred to it) lies in the carefully crafted interstices between Spanish and English. 'Garbage' translates directly as '*basura*', the latter reinforcing the former through repetition. But between 'I will not give them my voice' and '*Nunca les dare mi voz*' there is a key difference in emphasis: the Spanish text translates back as 'I will *never* give them my voice' – again reinforcement, but charged with a finality that subtly raises the stakes for the performer(s) delivering those lines (and for those audience members who understand both languages). Fuchs's dance of alienation and identification in the landscape of the text takes a further turn: if meaning is reinforced by repetition and growing emphasis in the first two instances of inter-linguistic approximation, '*Como noche sin fin*,' which translates as 'like endless night,' reinforces the preceding English 'Some are crying' through a process of poetic analogy. The effect is furthered by the juxtaposition 'never / endless' (*nunca / sin fin*), which fuses notions of finality and infinity, adding to the tragic dimension of the scene. More, the distance between the English and the Spanish words strengthens the feeling of '*desterrar*' to which Mayer-García has alluded, as though the languages themselves are being wrenched from one another. The position of the immigrant, or the refugee, living simultaneously in two worlds, constituted by different linguistic contexts, parallel universes, is physically expressed even in the positioning of the words on the page.

Thus, *Carthage/Cartagena* is a play in which the protagonist is in fact the text itself, this letter from afar, undergoing a peripeteia of winding verse, finding its way to its recipient, the reader/audience, engulfing them in the widening gap between what can and cannot be expressed. It begins with a prayer – the prayer of every poet who has found themselves confronted with the pain brought by the inadequacy of language:

> Man
> Dreams himself heaven
> He says
> Stars
> Can I speak?
> I want to learn
> A new language
> To return the one
> I lost
>
> (Opening, p. 101)

This prayer is repeated in the end, as a Coda, but now dubbed 'a prayer of transformation' (Coda, p. 131). The journey of the text is over, and like every journey, every odyssey, it has a transformative power. The words are the same, but their meaning has changed, sublimated by the act of writing, which offers echoes of a star-gazing Lorca, looking for hope amid the chaos of war. Svich borrows her lyricism from him – a writer with whom she has shared the intimacy of translation: indeed *Carta Ajena* could be staged *bajo la arena*, under the sand, as the Spanish poet would have it. This is the landscape of *Carthage*, where '[…] the horizon / bleeds sand / lines of continuous absence' (Canto Two, p. 108).

In SignDance Collective's approach, of course, the text is embodied. The human figure makes the landscape of words. For Heiner Müller, another writer with whom we may claim Svich has some affinity, and whose *Waterfront Wasteland Medea Material Landscape With Argonauts* also deals with the devastation of war, 'in every landscape, the I is collective […]' (Müller 1995: 46). If *Carta Ajena* is itself a protagonist who speaks in the first person, this is often the first person plural:

> We wait in silence in the gravel field with our hands tied
> And our heads to the ground.
> We wait for the other god voice to tell us who we are
> And what we must do.
> We wait.
>
> (Canto Five, p. 114)

And there are echoes, too, of a violent and yet hopeful Sarah Kane, certain that the human spirit, in spite of every holy terror fuck with which we bury ourselves, still finds the resilience to utter a kind word.

Fuck, he says. Fuck, I'm told.

Pierdo mi lengua…

I do.
I act (upon this other body I do not know who smells of cigarettes and acid wine.)
I come.
Prod. Up. Prod. Move. Other there, voice says.
And onto a field I am thrown.
A field of gravel fenced in. A nowhere place.

(Canto Five, p. 112)

And, later:

> Dissolve your body
> Glow inside my eyelids
> Cut open my veins there you will see
> I grace a time that will make me proud
> Yet my heart will be blasted always
> (Canto Five, p. 116)

'*Pierdo mi lengua*' means both 'I lose my language' and 'I lose my tongue.' Kane's *Cleansed* comes to mind (itself carrying echoes of *Titus Andonicus*, of course). The graphic nature of the language and the violence of the imagery conveyed reinforce the notion that the text itself is in conflict with its own lyricism. We are looking at the stars, while drowning in the muck and wallow. And, like in Kane's *Blasted*, there is a rift in space and time around halfway through the text. There, the explosion that ruptures the play in two, at the same time connects the war that is ravaging outside with the personal violence we have seen taking place in the hotel room where Ian and Cate are staying. In *Carthage*, although space and time are never continuous (even if they form a kind of 'quantum-continuum'), a shift can be perceived between Cantos Five and Six, as if a border has been crossed. Travelling in the opposite direction of Kane's text, where the magnitude of the violence increases, the violence in *Carthage* acquires a more domestic, geographically located dimension: we are in 'A New Country/Un Mundo Nuevo' (another poetic mistranslation, Canto Six, p. 119), which is decidedly American. Svich is a world-writer, both in scope and genealogy – she is of Cuban-Argentine-Spanish-Croatian descent – but she is also a New World-writer, keenly attuned to North-American reality, filtered through a Latino sensibility. Thus, the violence of war and human trafficking that is portrayed in the first half of *Carthage* is connected to the violence of dispossession, of 'murders un-remarked' (Canto Nine, p. 127), of cities full of steel and scarce friendship in the second half. A dystopian, impersonal American dream, which has, for people of Hispanic origin, an even further dimension of dislocation and abandonment. '*Pierdo mi lengua…*' Here, one is reminded, too, of Kane's *4:48 Psychosis*:

Languages surround me
new as Carthage ancient, as *Cartagena vieja*

and in the and in the and in the
twenty-five forty-one fifty fifty
one one one
light light light
twenty-five
six seventy and hit the
hit the
hit the
light light light
sign me sign me sign me to here
light
to here
light
light…
to where…

(Canto Six, p. 122)

And then, crucially, the text has something reminiscent of Samuel Beckett, aware of our absurd human condition. The Sisyphean boulder keeps coming back in the form of repeated words, actions, images – yet we keep pushing it up that hill. In 2002, Svich was already writing of

> a panic about where we will go next. If we are indeed going anywhere. The spectre of fascism, rises and our souls tremble at the thought of mistakes repeated, and civilizations lost. Everything is called into question. Doubt hangs in the air. Faith can no longer sustain us. If it ever did.
>
> (Svich 2002: 15)

Like Vladimir and Estragon in *Waiting for Godot*, we do not move. We are indeed buried in the sand, like Winnie in *Happy Days*. And, like these characters, we hope, we wait, we spend days waiting. But there is something even more fundamentally Beckettian in *Carthage*: assuming the role of protagonist, the text offers itself as the vehicle through which a world comes into being, and language becomes its midwife,

Almost god
Almost mouth
(Canto Five, p. 111)

This is as much *Not I* as it is *Godot*. Reading *Carthage* is constructing its narratives and unraveling its characters: these nameless, unknown soldiers, immigrants, and (sex) slaves, these figures undefined by any markers other than their words (kind or otherwise). Just as for the mouth in *Not I*, each utterance is an affirmation of being, brought about by the fact that there is an auditor there to listen. Here, this role is played by you, kind reader, or the audience who might watch a production of *Carthage*. This seemingly 'unstageable' piece of writing is therefore, in fact, fundamentally theatrical. It is an act of witnessing, being witnessed. I speak; therefore, I am. Again, Svich explains: 'The artist leaves an imprint, caught by the eye of the witness who is the audience' (2002: 16). The very existence of the text is, of course, also an act of resistance. By articulating the unbearable, the playwright takes the first step toward bridging the divide between what is and what might be. 'If the artist does not defend and advance sensibility in an age of violence and concern, then what is the role of the artist?', asks Svich in *Theatre in Crisis?* (2002: 16). The text as an act of healing, dealing with trauma.

In his important *Disability Aesthetics*, Tobin Siebers has a chapter dedicated to 'Trauma Art,' where he calls for an approximation of disability studies with trauma studies. The prevalence of images of violence in contemporary literature, theatre, visual arts, and media points toward an aesthetics of trauma that, Siebers claims, should embrace the notion of disability. He argues, 'Disability has emerged as a central aesthetic concept not only because it symbolises human variation, but also because it represents the fragility of human beings and their susceptibility to dramatic mental and physical change' (Siebers 2010: 102). This points toward a state of being in which uncertainty is key, and the stability of texts is subject to the contingencies of history. We could say that the text of *Carthage* is, in this way, disabled: it is its own protagonist, one with broken grammar, changeable syntax, uncertain characters and narrative. It is, certainly, dramatic. And as we have seen, in this landscape theatre, relations of causality in time are also compromised. Even so, Svich explores notions of memory and repression, associated with trauma; the word 'before' occurs 20 times in the text. Time is divided between the present and 'Before':

Before yes
Before
love
easy
Like rain
I did not even think

I just…
Stream
Empty
Like shopping

(Canto One, p. 105)

Returning, then, for a moment, to Fuchs's notion of landscape theatre, the play 'present[s] dispersed fields of activity where many time periods may be represented simultaneously' (Fuchs 1996: 12), and the very difficulty that accompanies an articulation of the past in the text brings it forcefully to the present of the reader/audience.

Nonetheless, and in spite of the absence of time frame – or perhaps their multiplicity – a possible key to unlocking narrative structure exists in the titles of the cantos themselves. After the opening prayer, which calls for a language to articulate the unspeakable, 'Canto One: Earth/Mundo' introduces the world of the play, which is of course the whole world, a 'Sorry patch earth this' (Canto One, p. 101), a world full of languages, and where fear reigns; 'Canto Two: Shelled' paints a picture of war and destruction, 'death-stained, death-marked / shattered' (Canto Two, p. 108). Still, this is a world that allows for memories of love, and memories of plans unfulfilled, curtailed by unspeakable violence. 'Canto Three: Cargo' depicts human figures as the spoils of war, being loaded into a container to be taken away:

> I am put
> Inside a large container
> Made of metal
> Shiny
> I cannot breathe
> They slit a whole
>
> (Canto Three, p. 109)

We are confronted with the text and its textures. The roughness of the situation contrasts with the shine of the metal. 'Canto Four: Voyage – *A donde vamos, a donde van*'[3] describes the horrors of the journey we undertake: 'stinks everyone piss shit everyone crying grunts moans sounds make quiet ropes in mouths chafing lips tongues bleeding tongues wanting water…love…and then and then piss numb skin' (Canto Four, p. 110), until the text arrives at 'Canto Five: Station.' In this, the longest canto in the play, the figures are at a border station, a waiting post, holding pen, detention center. The place is undetermined, but memories and dreams/reveries remove us from wherever we are and from the trauma of the present, in which violence and sexual abuse take place. Indeed, up until now, we could have been in Srebrenica, Dresden, Damascus, or Fallujah; Auschwitz or Abu Ghraib; in a holocaust train, in the back of a truck, or in the bowels of a slave-ship.

The subject in the sentences from the paragraph above keeps shifting; be assured, kind reader, that I am aware of this: the cantos, the human figures, we, the text – all are interchangeable. In this *Carta Ajena*, the letter, its contents, the writer, and the readers (and performers and audiences) all become metonymical accomplices. 'I cannot breathe' (Canto Three, p. 109), says the text, and the audience hold their breath. Svich acknowledges that '[t]he place where writing begins is a pure one. It is an intense, electric silence where we meditate deep within ourselves, and breathe through the pen or pencil, and leave the circle of our breath on the page' (Svich 2002: 19). Bearing witness to a history automatically inserts the witness into that history.

It is at this point that the text (and we with it) crosses a border. We have reached breaking point, and the whole weight of that history, which was witnessed by the first five cantos, forces *Carthage/Cartagena* to fold into itself. 'Canto Six: A New Country/Un Mundo Nuevo,' as mentioned before, brings us to the New World. We are in America, where yet another dream/reverie takes place – even if '[n]othing is what I want it to be' (Canto Six, p. 120). This is also the Mexican border, and this moment points toward the Ciudad Juárez of Svich's *Iphigenia Crash Land Falls on the Neon Shell That Was Once Her Heart* (2012). The 'narcos' are never far away. The horrors do not exclusively exist in a foreign (to Anglophone audiences) Cartagena: Carthage is in America, too. Thus, 'Canto Seven: Before' is a longing back to a time before speech, when 'I was / Whole' (Canto Seven, p. 124). The structure of the verse is of course ambiguous:

Before
Before
Speech

(Canto Seven, p. 123)

Is this really a time before speech, or a before-time, in which there was speech, when language was understood? In either case, the now-time is seen to bring about a splitting of the self, in a Lacanian twist that encapsulates one of the paradoxes of *Carta Ajena*: language is at the same time midwife and executioner; it both unites and divides.

'Canto Eight: The Blinking World' complements this notion. Here, the text embraces its designation of canto, and acquires distinctly song-like characteristics, with echoes of spirituals, scraps of lyrics collaged together. A voice in Spanish states: '*canto ahora porque no me queda más que cantar* [...] *canto porque canto; porque eso es lo que quieren, verdad?*' (Canto Eight, p. 125).[4] The paradox of the text is the self-same paradox of song, at once comforting and sorrowful.

It is in Canto Eight, too, that we have perhaps the brightest glimmer of hope present in the whole text. A moment of compassion and generosity in this unrelenting play: 'Brother, I greet you with open arms. I offer you my frailties / The deep down chaos that makes me breathe' (Canto Eight, p. 126). And yet, in a powerful instance of the imbrication of text, performance, writer, and audiences alluded to above; the passage that includes these kind words is preceded by the following 'unstageable' stage direction:

(Hidden track, words heard as if a page has been torn out of a book.)

(Canto Eight, p. 125)

What is being read, played, spoken, or witnessed? And by whom? It seems that even the very pages in which *Carta Ajena* becomes a compassionate letter are violently removed from the text itself, distended from history. 'Canto Nine: Six Moves Across A Field / Touch down America' is a piece of Americana. Divided in six parts, or moves, it journeys through a United States that is laden with images of homelessness, violence, wild weather, and religion. A journey that begins with an escape:

> This is how we leave
> Out the back door
>
> (Canto Nine: one, p. 126)

However, a complete withdrawal is impossible:

> Cause we know we're
> Never more than a stone's throw away
> From a place and time
> Where we all we got is learning and forgetting
> And watching the space between me and you
> And You and me
>
> (Canto Nine: three, p. 127)

The journey ends with a set of questions:

> What can be done with this
> Lonesome child
> Adrift in your backyards
> In your fever America
> What can be done
>
> (Canto Nine: six, pp. 130–31)

The absence of punctuation challenges the perception that this is a question. Still, the answer, once again, lies in memory, in before-time. And so, 'Canto Ten: Before' is reminiscent of the homonymous Canto Seven; here, though, the self is not split, but emptied:

> Before
> Before
> Me
>
> […]
>
> But then
> But then
> Desert
> I became
>
> (Canto Ten, p. 131)

The desertification of the self is the ultimate journey that the text undertakes – yet the 'I' persists. In Fuchs's landscapes 'the human figure is no longer the measure of all things' (Fuchs 1996: 12). In them, 'the human figure, instead of providing perspectival unity to a stage whose setting acts as a backdrop and visual support, is treated as an element in what might be described as a theatrical landscape' (Fuchs 1996: 92). This is perhaps where Svich's text deviates from the notion proposed by Fuchs. Her theatre in general, and *Cartagena* in particular, remains fundamentally human. Language is gone; the self is gone; humanity remains. At the end of Canto Ten, all that is left is a figure who

> *[…] tries to speak. The words don't come. The figure tries and tries.*
> *The body struggles to catch the sounds that erupt from within: living vestiges, bastard*
> *remains of the before self inscribed in the body and voice –*
> *Gasps, hollers, stuttering consonants, choked breaths, cries, yelps…*
> *From memory held;*
> *A scream.*
>
> (p. 131)

And the coda of a prayer, the same prayer that started the journey, in a different, and yet the same time and place. A double. To be sure, Antonin Artaud's 'The Theatre and Its Double' (1974) provides a valuable framework with which to engage with *Carthage*. Consider the stage direction above, in light of this passage from 'The Theatre of Cruelty (First Manifesto),' in which Artaud proposes a stage language 'consisting of the accumulation of all the impulsive gestures, all the abortive postures, all the lapses in the mind and of the tongue by which speech's incapabilities are revealed' (Artaud 1974: 72). His desire for this 'cruel' stage language, capable of expressing the inexpressible through movement, gesture, and sound, is materialized here. The writer of 'Production and Metaphysics' was

> well aware that a language of gestures and postures, dance and music is less able to define character, to narrate man's thoughts, to explain conscious states clearly and exactly, than spoken language. But whoever said theatre was made to define character, to resolve conflicts of a human, emotional order, of a present-day, psychological nature such as those which monopolise contemporary theatre?
>
> (Artaud 1974: 28)

Indeed, starting from its very title, *Carthage/Cartagena* is full of 'doubles.' On a surface level, as I have pointed out (and quite obviously), there is the opening prayer, repeated as coda; Cantos Seven and Ten; the first, 'world' part of the text and the second, American half; the English and Spanish languages. But also, at the level narrative and character, inasmuch as these elements can be identified in the text: before-time and now; memory and hope; reality and dream; kindness and cruelty; victims and perpetrators. There is an instance in Canto Five that epitomizes this: 'Nana is my other self. *Mi otro yo.*' (p. 113). We are in a memory, simultaneously in before-time and now, and crossing the border between two languages. A speaker who sees her- or himself in the past, dreaming of a future where they will 'be like Nana and make apricot cakes' (Canto Five, p. 113). A double mirror of time and otherness. Moreover, in SignDance Collective's staging, those two sentences are shared by two performers who had been seen acting as oppressor and oppressed, the aggressor hankering back to his childhood, the victim becoming the Spanish-speaking grandmother. Rather than being resolved, conflicts are complicated; rather than being defined, characters are comingled.

In fact, every character/performer is each other's double in some way, at some point. The notion that the perpetrator of unspeakable aggression may begin as, become, or even at one and the same time be a victim highlights the eternal and universal (time and space, as symbolized by the many incarnations of Carthage) cycle of human violence. Judith Butler, speaking at the 2014 PEN World Voices Festival of International Literature, suggests that 'Perhaps in destroying, one insists that the rest of the world become mired in one's own sense of devastation' (Butler 2014). The stories are not linear, and relations of cause and consequence are blurred, in processes of loss and transformation. The logical implication of this is that the idea of the double is not exclusively binary. There is a more complex web of grief, rage, and interdependency in operation. Butler tells us that 'before [that word again] ever losing, we are lost in the other, lost without the other' (Butler 2014). Take, for example, these figures from movement 'five' of Canto Nine:

> Here's a man of no fixed address
> Addressing you
> Addressing himself
> In this fixed America of the free
> And dispossessed
>
> [...]
>
> Here's a woman
> asking what all happened here
> In this curved world
> Scratched out
>
> [...]
>
> Here's a swollen child
> Who appears in the day's rain
> with levelled eyes
> and a blown head
>
> [...]
>
> you there with that smile
> And your hand wrapped

In a river of feeling
Isn't it funny how we both are
Pretty
Sad
De-created
For who made us

(Canto Nine: five, pp. 129–30)

Man, woman, and child – all are each other's intersubjective double; and finally, fundamentally: the text and you, kind reader. Artaud, in 'Alchemist Theatre' proclaims that 'true theatre, just like poetry but by other means, is born from organised anarchy' (Artaud 1974: 36). Caridad Svich embraces this notion fully in her work, in the craft of her carefully constructed art. The third play in this volume, *The Orphan Sea*, is eminently poetic; and if the first play in this book is called *JARMAN (all this maddening beauty)*, one could also say that *Carthage* has a kind of beautiful madness. This is not a naive aestheticizing of violence, but an acknowledgment that there is something about our common humanity that is simultaneously powerful and incredibly fragile, like a state of mind 'half mad with forgiveness / and a memory from Before time' (Canto Five, p. 115).

The presentation of anarchy, chaos, and war challenges us aesthetically, ethically, and historically, at a time when ugly nationalisms are re-emerging across Europe; when at the same time nation-states are being supplanted and undermined by international financial organizations, supra-national terrorist organizations, multinational corporations. 'It takes every bit of you to be good, it takes every kind of strength there is,' says a voice in Canto Eight (p. 126). Butler seems to agree: 'Peace is […] the practice of resisting the terrible satisfactions of war' (Butler 2014). Here lies the drama of *Carthage*.

In the noise of war
In the whisper of a brother who is no longer
The country crowns itself in my delusion
The confessions of a wayward son have been taken down
(Canto Five, p. 116)

And soon after:

poco a poco, poco a poco, nos olividaremos de todo y de nada; por mi patria, por mi patria, por mi puta patria[5]

(Canto Five, p. 116)

Carthage, Cartagena, *Carta Ajena*, a letter from afar. The personal and textual geographies and histories of Caridad Svich's play get mixed up in a world where languages intermingle and nothing is really stable.

In the end it is we who surrender.

References

Artaud, A. (1974), 'The Theatre and Its Double', in *Collected Works, Volume Four* (trans. V. Corti), London: John Calder, pp. 1–110.

Babbage, F. (2009), 'Heavy Bodies, Fragile Texts: Stage Adaptation and the Problem of Presence', in *Adaptation in Contemporary Culture: Textual Infidelities*, R. Carroll (ed.), London: Continuum, pp. 11–22.

Butler, J. (2014), 'On the Edge (of Upheaval)' [video], At *Opening Night of PEN World Voices*, http://www.pen.org/opening-night-pen-world-voices-judith-butler-video. Accessed 25 February 2015.

Fuchs, E. (1996), *The Death of Character: Perspectives on Theater after Modernism*, Bloomington and Indianapolis: Indiana University Press.

Laera, M. (2014), *Theatre and Adaptation: Return, Rewrite, Repeat*, London: Bloomsbury.

Machon, J. (2011), *(Syn)aesthetics: Redefining Visceral Performance*, Basingstoke: Palgrave Macmillan.

Mayer-García, E. (2014), '2014 *NoPassport Theatre Conference* Field Report', http://nopassport.org/blog/csvich/04/06/eric-mayer-garcia-2014-nopassport-theatre-conference-field-report, Accessed 25 February 2015.

Müller, H. (1995), *Theatremachine* (trans. and ed. M. von Henning), London and Boston: Faber and Faber.

Parks, S. (1994), 'The Death of the Last Black Man in the Whole Entire World', in *The America Play and Other Works,* New York: Theatre Communications Group, pp. 99–132.

Pavis, P. (1992), *Theatre at the Crossroads of Culture*, London and New York: Routledge.

Siebers, T. (2010), *Disability Aesthetics*, Ann Arbor: University of Michigan Press.

Svich, C. (2002), 'Theatre in Crisis? Living Memory in an Unstable Time', in *Theatre in Crisis? Performance Manifestos for a New Century*, M. Delgado and C. Svich (eds), Manchester: Manchester University Press, pp. 15–19.

Svich, C. (2003), 'The Dynamics of Fractals: Legacies for a New Tomorrow', in *Trans-Global Readings: Crossing Theatrical Boundaries*, C. Svich (ed.), Manchester: Manchester University Press, pp. 1–14.

Svich, C. (2013), 'A Reflection on The Other Side of the Coin by SignDance Collective International', in *Disability Arts Online*, http://www.disabilityartsonline.org.uk/sign-dance-collective-international-the-other-side-of-the-coin-NYC. Accessed 25 February 2015.

Notes

1 *The Other Side of the Coin*, devised by the company, with my dramaturgical input, was first performed in October 2012 at the Kulturwerstatt in Graz, Austria; it has since been performed in the United Kingdom (multiple venues), Austria, Slovenia, United States (multiple venues), Turkey, and Holland. For more information about the company, please see http://www.signdancecollectiveinternational.com/.

2   The 2014 *NoPassport Conference,* curated by Svich and co-curated by Mayer-Garcia, took place at Louisiana State University on 29 March. Its title was 'Dreaming the Americas: the Diasporic Imagination.' SignDance Collective performed a work-in-progress version of *Carthage/Cartagena,* directed by Beatriz Cabur, with choreography by Isolte Ávila and music by Lila Schwammerlin.
3   'Where are we going, where are they going' [My translation].
4   'I sing now because all there is left for me is to sing […] I sing because I sing; because this is what they want, right?' [My translation].
5   'Little by little, little by little, we will forget everything and nothing; for my country, for my country, for my fucking country' [My translation].

Carthage/Cartagena: when I looked up I looked for something (call it hope)
Ten cantos and a prayer for performance

Caridad Svich

Opening: A prayer

(In low light, a figure is revealed. A prayer.)

Man
Dreams himself heaven
He says
Stars
Can I speak?
I want to learn
A new language
To return the one
I lost

Canto One: Earth/Mundo

Sorry patch earth this
Mundo a-drowned in the muck and wallow
what here to move?
What here to lose?
Scraps
Throat-songs
Laid low
For fear
In fear
Of being catched
By those who They

Fear reigns in this sorry earth
In this *miedo mierdero* stained patch

I look up
Pa' arriba
I seek to move

Ahora
I let the earth follow me in tiny waves

Spit

What here to move?
In this land
Carthage
Ancient land
In this land
Cartagenas
Ancient land
Taken over by…

All here to lose

I make a circle
Alrededor del mundo
In earth's stain
I tell myself Pray
A los santos, a los dioses, a quien quiera escuchar

But words don't make
(don't) Reach
To heaven
El cielo se aparta

Words
Stay
Low
In ground
Rumble

I hear them
They wish for burial
Quick
Distend me from history
(They say)
Release me from all

But I cannot
Grant (such things)
I am human

Carthage/Cartagena

Figure 5: Performer Isolte Avila in *Carthage/Cartagena* open-air workshop, Graz, Austria (2014). Produced by Signdance Collective International © Brigitte Elser.

I am mere
Solo un pobre, una pobre
Un crimen ser pobre aqui
It is curse perhaps
To be
Mere
But such is what I am

So I listen
I let rumble keep on
I take rumble in me
I don't let on

No one knows, you see
That I keep words

(their wishes)
inside

Everyone thinks I'm
Nadie nada

Some think
garbage
They say this to me
Basura

I do not answer
I take the word in
I make it garbage
I put it to trash

…

In time
En hora buena
Words will refuse me
Will seek other shelter
Another body to keep
I know this
Even when not in prayer
Even when circle makes mess
When earth cannot take

Much war in this Carthage,
In this Cartagenas,
So much seen
Felt
In air

I hear things
Voices called up
Languages
De otras partes
I do not understand

I make sense
Where none is
I seek reason

I do
Because
Cursed perhaps
Human yes
On earth
Reckoned by reckoning
By ancients
Before
Before me
Before I was
Aligned
I was
Whole

But then
But then
Splintered
I became

…

earth shudders
earth blooms
speak
it says
pray,
it says
love

No puedo

Before yes
Before
love
easy
Like rain
I did not even think

I just…
Stream
Empty
Like shopping

This word I used most of all
Shopping
What does it mean now?

Thought consumes
It begs answer

I wait
I spend days waiting
Sometimes shopping is all I want
When windows black and smashed

I think about things
Crave
Candy, toys, spinning tops, *bocaditos de leche*….
Things of childhood

I could sell such things
I could make a living

My father
Before me
Mi papa sold
In one year he sold two thousand items
He made a killing
He used that word
Killing

I don't use that word
Earth stained, you see

…

I make a circle
Alrededor del mundo
Again/*Otra vez*
Like ancients
I pray
I wait.

Canto Two: Shelled

Beneath a pile of shells
I pretend I'm dead
I wait for the gunfire to stop

but it won't
not here
Not in Carthage

a border's length away
even the imitation of gunfire
can be heard

I wriggle under the shells
I dream of Hakim when he was alive
his cologne on my skin
now bloodied
upon me

Hakim dances here with me
in waking sleep
in death's pretense
The border falls between us
between Carthage…
and the memory of another ancient city

I sing to him in an old language
the language of stars and signs
the language that begs questions

                                          Man
                        Dreams himself heaven
                                  He says
                                     Stars
                              Can I speak?

We conjure
visions of Australia
red desert
far away
marked by lines of song
and voices un-vanished.

                              I want to learn
                              A new language
                                To return…

I lie under shells
metal-cased

Leave me dead
I say
Leave me to the dead

                                                                       The one
                                                                            I lost

Here the horizon
bleeds sand
lines of continuous absence

Leave me to the dead
I say

Do not find me
I whisper

Leave me here
death-stained, death-marked
shattered

                                                                        The one
                                                                            I lost

You border me
Reinscribe terror
Border me
with wires and chains
with lines in the sand
that will vanish one day.

I resist.

Leave me to the dead
I say
Leave me

I am called mad.
I am trade.
Human vessel. Cargo.

You will not be left
They say.

I am stripped
I am told Write Eastward
East breaks
under my pen.
It refuses space
for ink
Gasoline envelopes the world.

Keep on
They say.

Too soon East will splinter its voice
Too soon I will splinter
Traded I will be for the price of a simple pen.

Only Hakim's memory
will hold me.
The memory of his skin…

Canto Three: Cargo

I am put
Inside a large container
Made of metal
Shiny
I cannot breathe
They slit a hole

They say
This will do

They tie me

Do not move
They say

Wire cuts into my skin.
I want to scream
But I don't
I will not give them my voice

Nunca les dare mi voz

They do not look at me
They do not see me
I am garbage to them

Basura

But trade nonetheless

In the container
There are others
Tied, too
Silent, too
Some are crying

Como noche sin fin

I do not look at anyone
I stay within
My skin bleeds
It is cold
Soon I will hear nothing
but

Canto Four: Voyage
A donde vamos, a donde van

fuck God holy god fuck
Fuck fuck fuck where
This here where this here fuck tell me where please this
crying.

…

Tears fuck hold piss down tears come can't stop can't crying like baby baby where's my baby sweet baby S sweet baby child hold me hold me hold in ground shrapnel baby…fuck

…

stinks everyone piss shit everyone crying grunts moans sounds make quiet ropes in mouths chafing lips tongues bleeding tongues wanting water…love…and then and then piss numb skin

…

We're going to the country, he says
To a place with pink walls and lemon trees, he says
It will be beautiful, he says
You'll see.

…

I want to believe. I want to pray. I want to have faith.
But I do not believe anything. Anymore.

                                          I know now this is the first step of dying…

Shouts all over Screams outside where where where we are where tell me tell do not tell do not speak quiet quiet stop listen no listen pray no pray stop feeling what feeling empty feeling piss feeling screw feeling fuck it fuck it fuck it fuck god holy terror fuck I can't see do be anything but trash

And then in quiet, in silence

A voice heard
A leg pulled
Come on, he says
Let's go, he says. Out.

Canto Five: Station

Pushed into van, tied hands, feet numb, huddled amongst bodies I wait

                                            Crushed together pressed
                                                        Almost god
                                                       Almost mouth

For my number for my new name to be created from this other god voice
I do not know

                                                        Almost god
                                                       Almost mouth

I wait as in voyage in holy terror fuck permanent state
I do not recall Before it is hidden now buried
I am only object now to be moved, sold, made for trade

Merest human I reckon
But there is no reckoning here
Van stops. Door swings wide. Day in eyes. What day is this?
No questions here. Just listen. To the other god voice
It says You. It says Up. Prod. I am moved. I am handed to another body.
I am told Fuck. I am told Fuck.
I'm shaking. Hit. Stop. Hit. The other body waits for me.
Fuck, he says. Fuck, I'm told.

Pierdo mi lengua…

I do.
I act (upon this other body I do not know who smells of cigarettes and acid wine.)
I come.
Prod. Up. Prod. Move. Other there, voice says.
And onto a field I am thrown.
A field of gravel fenced in. A nowhere place.
A field of men who kneel, hands bound, legs crunched,
with their faces against the sky.
I do the same. I mimic.
I hear the van pull away.

I wait as in voyage in holy terror fuck permanent state
I think of nothing but here this wherever this may be hot, dry place
The field of men is silent.
I pray for rain. I stop myself from praying.
I know this is not to be done now. Not even in silence.
I want to look up, but I don't. Sky promise gone. Sky promise false.
Must believe this now. To keep from screaming. To keep from dying.

> This is when I knew it was the second step of
> dying…

I am like everyone else. I must be like everyone else.
The quiet man will survive.

> If he is quiet…

The field expands. Gravel sticks. Heat burns my brain.
A dream overtakes me:

Pink walls and lemon trees.

A country house. Children playing. I am six.
It is my birthday. Nana has made an apricot cake.
Dusted sugar cookies for the crust. You will eat, she says.
Her voice is warm. It sings of long nights of love. It speaks mystery.
I never think where did Nana come from?
Nana just is. She must've sprung straight from the earth like this
Giving and smiling and making cake for birthday.
Nana's husband died in a war. She never talks about him, the husband gone.
He is mystery too. Faded photograph on a wall. A formal pose.
We ask questions sometimes, but Nana doesn't answer.
She looks up. At the sky. Promise there for her. We sense this
And we learn from her. We imitate. Sky is for promise.
Good sons, good children we are.
Nana cuts a piece of cake. She offers it. She sings a private song.

>'They went south to find the rain
>They went north to stave off pain
>They never ever did complain
>Of being lost.
>
>Oh joyous men of war-like days
>Oh splendid men whom we praise
>How can it be, how can it be
>You are gone.'

Nana is my other self. *Mi otro yo*. I know this. Even when I'm six.
One day I will be like Nana and make apricot cakes
And sing songs to myself that everyone can hear, I say.
Silly child, she says. Why are you such a silly child?
Come here, little one, give me a kiss.

Memory saves....

The clouds rush. For a moment, it seems as if rain, but only
More heat.

Stinging, affectless, burning...

(for) time uncounted.
No calendar here.
There's only sunup. And sunfall.

And for some no sun at all.
Some of the men here are hooded.
Have been for some time (I later find out)

Later later much later
After…

These men have lost all sense of light.

Pity escapes breath
Ah

We wait in silence in the gravel field with our hands tied
And our heads to the ground.
We wait for the other god voice to tell us who we are
And what we must do.
We wait.

Esperamos para el fin de dias sin descanso, dias sin sonrisa ni brisa, dias de angustia y poca luz, por mi patria, por mi patria, por mi puta patria

Three suns pass and the other god voice speaks.
It is accompanied by other god voices who kick our legs and order us to move.
We are going someplace. A party, voices say.
We will be asked to entertain guests.
Look smart. Smile. Be ready.
We do not know what this means.
The hooded men are held back. They won't be part of the party.
We, the lucky (to think I can think this word, but yes, lucky to still be)
move forward. One god voice unties my hands.
For a moment, I think I will be released,

To where
Past graveled death

but instead
A different cord is wrapped
Round wrists and through fingers laced.
More durable, voice says.

Do I recognize this voice?
For no more than a split second

I think yes
A flash of memory

De mi pueblo, de la esquina, voz calida del mar

And smile, voice says.
You will be posing for a picture.

Give me a look.
A look and look, as if calm,
a look that is looking through the eye,
the soul looking through the eye
like a message sent by matter,
show me your purposeless orb…

The party will begin soon.

A rush of air
A voice from another time
A messenger is heard
Light bends
A song is heard against a creeping red sky
half mad with forgiveness
and a memory from Before time

The last party I went to was too loud and too fast. I remember thinking when will this night ever end and not wanting to tell anyone I was tired because everyone wanted to have such a good time. We must've drunk several bottles of wine and the place reeked of different kinds of smoke. There were friends everywhere but also strangers. People I'd never seen. Tourists, someone said. I thought how strange that there are tourists at my friend's party, but I said nothing because everyone was trying so hard to have a good time. I went out to the patio and the paper lanterns shimmered in the moonlight. I felt out of time. As if I were in a movie.

He disappears in a B-movie dream
With a voice as dry as the desert
Gunshot overlay
A scorched flag
What mem'ry here?

Hakim was somewhere else inside. I pretended I was the only person left on earth and tried to see if I could see past the yard up through the hills and into the next country and wondered if there were parties going on there too and what they were like.

> In the noise of war
> In the whisper of a brother who is no longer
> The country crowns itself in my delusion
> The confessions of a wayward son have been taken down
> The spores of the sky whirl
> Spare not the undoing of an age
> What mem'ry this?

Someone came up behind me. A friend. A hug dizzy with drink, and I turned away and forgot about the next country for a while.

> A rush of air
> A voice from another time
> A messenger is heard
> Light bends
> A song is heard against a creeping red sky
> half mad with forgiveness
> Chew dirt
> Half passed out
> The earth sighs upon a craving spirit

In this new place we are taken everything is gray. The walls are hard
And the party is in full sway. Everyone is wearing black and white and shades of gray and acts as if they are somewhere else. Exaggerated gestures, wide laughs, and voices pitched high.

> Dissolve your body
> Glow inside my eyelids
> Cut open my veins there you will see
> I grace a time that will make me proud
> Yet my heart will be blasted always

We are made to stand against the walls and smile. We are made to observe.

> I offer you a mirror of spun glass
> So you may observe your frailty
> And beg to weep

Noches de parada, sin decanso, tiesos, respirando a pocas; sonrisas aplastadas a nuestra caras, disfigurando nuestros rostros, cambiando nuestro idioma; poco a poco, poco a poco, nos olividaremos de todo y de nada; por mi patria, por mi patria, por mi puta patria

Figure 6: Performer Francesca Osimani in *Carthage/Cartagena* open-air workshop, Graz, Austria (2014). Produced by Signdance Collective International © Brigitte Elser.

On occasion during the night, we are made to service the guests in gray rooms
And are asked to fake prayer. I think of Nana's birthday cake when I was six
And try not to think of anything else as I am posed for another and another picture.

Against the inner caul of the earth
They fight for possession
of something that belongs to neither of them
This is a prophecy.
It is writ in a book.
'Everyone will be slain but one will be left standing.'
Your body
is at the edge of heaven.

Man
Dreams himself
heaven

> Fury unleashed in still repose.

Flash in eyes.
Pictures taken.
Party shuts down.
Lights out.

And we're shoved into another van now.
Transported elsewhere. Location unknown.

> Keening. In quiet time.
> The sound of keening sustains me.

(reverie)

You.

Tu.

It was…

Eras…

My head is spinning.

> *Quieres…?*

Si.

You want…?

Siempre.

> I don't think I can…

Give.

…

What about me?

You've no choice, .

I had once. I had everything.

A moment becomes an eternity.

                                                                         I won't sleep. Not ever.

I can't even remember myself.

…

Put your hand inside me.

What are you made of?

Scrap metal and wretched eyes that blink and weep.

There are shadows, dancing on the concrete.

…

                                Hold onto me.

We're far away now. We're almost

                                                                             in
                                                                             the
                                                                      country.

Surrender your eyes.

There will be nothing left if we keep on like this.

                                (Silence.)

The languages change.
The other god voices fade.

Canto Six: A New Country/Un Mundo Nuevo

Light bends
A song is heard against a yellow sky

                                                                half mad with forgiveness

I chew dirt

                                            Against the inner caul of the earth

I find my way
Again.

(2nd reverie)

When I look at you, when you batter me, when sound falls and we're left

                                                            Nothing is what it…

Nothing is what I want it to be.

                                  Liquid angels.

Liquid dreams.

No crying on an empty belly.

                                            I give myself a cold, hard fist.

Something shatters.

                                                      Inside I am weak.

My strength is fading.

How many lives in this life?

How many days until I see you again?

Is that what you dream?

                                      I think nothing else. I am consumed.

I've no shame left. Everything has descended.
I can be empty.

Everyone's dead now. Gone to purgatory.

To a yellow ocean.

With yellow sand, and yellow fish with sick fins.

> *Donde mandan a las que cruzan el paso de los narcos de las Cartas- ajenas*

…The other day

I was walking

And I felt your cry in my throat.

> *Breath breath breath breath breath breath breath breath…………………………………..*

The hardest thing to do is let go.

Give everything up?

Give everything away.

…

The world is thin. It evaporates in my hands.

Everything's loose.

It's all earth now.

We'll eat.

We'll become large.

And nobody will want to rescue us because we will be giants.

(Silence.)

I am caught once again
into the human.

Untied
Released
Half-mad
unknown

I am escaped unto myself

Cut open in a new world

                                                The man mourns his former self
                                                          This is a prophecy.
                                                        It is writ in a book.
                                                 'Everyone will be slain
                                                                but one
                                                              will be left
                                                                 standing.'

This I tell myself is the first step toward living

                                       The man mourns what he's left behind
                                                  The spores of the sky whirl

Languages surround me
new as Carthage ancient, as *Cartagena vieja*

                     and in the and in the and in the
                        twenty-five forty-one fifty fifty
                                one one one
                               light light light
                                  twenty-five
                        six seventy and hit the
                                    hit the
                                    hit the
                             light light light
                sign me sign me sign me to here
                                      light
                                   to here
                                      light
                                     light…
                                 to where…

I make my way
despite

                                                      Every hand lunatic
                                                  Membrane rupture
                                          whisper grunt rattle moan

The city opens in my orbiting eyes

    Que ciudad esta? Llena de acero, llena de pocos amigos (como dicen)
        Ciudad de desamparo

                    Look at that one
                         They say
                            Look

The buildings quiver. The lights come on.
(as if petals were loose inside me)

                      Look at that one
                      That one's a…a…

I'm a

        Men in suits racing to meet their next and next
          Dogs on leashes straining their masters
      Women in fake fur getting out of long black cars

I'm a

                                    Hah.

Kick it, swear it, punch it, nail it.
Scream.

            Litter one on the street
            Shatter one on a grave
    A half-blaze around a doorframe and calling
      'Split and release, split and release.'

Canto Seven: Before

Before
Before
Speech

Before
Before I was

Aligned
I was
Whole

But now
But now

No swear
Left in me…

Canto Eight: The Blinking World

away from everything
that rankles and rancors,
sweats and bothers,
furrows the brow
wrinkles the wrinkle;
oh praise hosanna

                                                  wouldn't that be divine:

I give up the mighty ghost
to another self

                                                        in another country

without baggage

                              'Oh say don't you know can you see him?
                                He's coming on the down-bound train.
                                      He's got shells in his hands
                                          And a pocket full of rye
                                  And he's coming to take you away
                                              All glory. Hallelujah.
                            He's coming on the down-bound train.'

I sing goodbye to my burning city
I sing bye bye Miss Acid Hula Pie

                                                  Like old song heard once
                                                     On a battered radio

Carthage/Cartagena

Canto sin pena, porque ya no la tengo, se me fue, en un barco, etre unas manos, atadas; en un campo frio al aire libre sin libertad; canto ahora porque no me queda más que cantar; vendo mi canto al quien lo compre; más alla de la sonrisa y brutalidad de mi linda Cartagena, de mi Carthage vieja; canto porque canto; porque eso es lo que quieren, verdad?

I sing
Rain rain,
Lluvia, lluvia y mas lluvia

Slaughter,
And more slaughter.

No rest for the rain.
It has work to do.
Listen.

shhhhh…
like the grass.

And
a crack of light.

in the release of plenty,
let beauty be unbound.

I hold it in my hands
with sweet breath
and strong fist

The sleep of day
Awakens the man to reason
Come through slaughter
And look upon tired hands
The cries of a sweet child
Heard upon a soul grieving

Where is my Carthage now?

    (Hidden track, words heard as if a page has been torn out of a book.)

Remember above all things, brother, that to live is not difficult
It takes no more than a bit of courage and a little ease
You ride on the wing, you nestle down, you never stay too long in one place

Remember, brother, when you're tossing about,
when pain wrecks the better part of you,
That to be a good person, to come through slaughter,
to keep hold of all your demons
When the world is not right, not even close,
Is more than anything
It takes every bit of you to be good, it takes every kind of strength there is

Brother, I greet you with open arms. I offer you my frailties
The deep down chaos that makes me breathe
This is not easy, this is not what should be
But grant me this, sweet night, quiet breath, tongue of light,
Do not forget, never forget, what it is to be human, what it is to fail,
What it is to bury yourself in hate,
And live in a land that is addicted to plenty and just rewards.

Take off your armor, save yourself, protect your integrity.
This is what I say to you, brother, from the silence that surrounds us
From the page that vanishes from my hands as I try to touch it.
Hold on, I say, save yourself, then after a moment, go back to before
To a time you cannot imagine
And in that time think about when there wasn't a murmur on this planet
And all was

Canto Nine: Six Moves Across A Field/ Touch down America

one

This is how we leave
Out the back door
With not a stitch
And whatever fits
In the gym bag
We haven't used for gym in a long time

With our hearts in our throats
And our chins high
Pushing pedal to the metal
Hitching a ride

Without a thought
Of forgiveness
In this strange playground
That lets devils
Roam freely
And grifters get by
On the easy mark

With rough noise
And a song pitched high
This is how we leave

two

And we don't even think about

What foul weather we come across
In furious Georgia
And ghostly Utah
And hell-bent Arkansas

What second mind dictates
The collapsible fury
Of crimes undetected
And murders un-remarked

What child holds a candle
To light
And whose memory befalls
The silent surveyor
Of all gone
We don't even think about

three

Cause we know we're
Never more than a stone's throw away
From a place and time
Where we all we got is learning and forgetting
And watching the space between me and you
And You and me

In the current flicker of morning
Left. Bereft. Standing.
A shadow score.
A body held tight.
Held by fear
And tears
Unshed.

four

This is what we say
As we count desire
As we escape vengeance
And scrape by
The mystery of fact

This here is not where I'm from
This here is outrage
Felt in the bone
Of the adopted brother who was born here
And told she was not from here
But from
That other
Amnesia
Of signs
From Some other
Fixed ecology
Of yearning
Whose devices
We record
In the absence
Of feeling
We prize

Ask me forgiveness
Ask me jesus
What all you done
To make so many use you clean
What all you is
that
makes you an easy mark

For the trickster angels
To play with

five

Here's a man of no fixed address
Addressing you
Addressing himself
In this fixed America of the free
And dispossessed
Unpossessed of words that can excuse
Betrayal
Shaped from flesh to ghost and back again
Stranded in a national dream
Of past-times
And half-times
And cheers and shouts
And good ol time
pummel-wide
Hard
And let me down NOT EASY

Here's a woman
asking what all happened here
In this curved world
Scratched out
A bullet hole
A scrape
fire lit
Balanced in the sky
Burning words
Hardened by luck
And the design of chance

Here's a swollen child
Who appears in the day's rain
with leveled eyes
and a blown head
blown with thought
and a hunger for apples
cider ripe

This child bears fruit
child song
Work song
Sorrow song
Joy song

A ballad
Woven by long thin hands of bony silver
That kick back dandelions and weeds

That shoot care out the window
Out the door
And say:
Come here, fella
Spank-whap, hey-slap
look over your shoulder

you there with that smile
And your hand wrapped
In a river of feeling
Isn't it funny how we both are
Pretty
Sad
De-created
For who made us

And How we don't think now
bout
Low light
On a Friday morning
And how this is
How we got to see the world

six

Ain't love a blunder
Ain't it kind
Oh love tempt
Take me in honey
Without a name

What can be done with this
Lonesome child

Adrift in your backyards
In your fever America
What can be done

Canto Ten: Before

Before
Before
Me

Before
Before
Re-
Re-member
I was
Whole

But then
But then
Desert
I became

The figure tries to speak. The words don't come. The figure tries and tries.
The body struggles to catch the sounds that erupt from within: living vestiges, bastard remains
of the before self inscribed in the body and voice –
Gasps, hollers, stuttering consonants, choked breaths, cries, yelps…
From memory held;
A scream.
And then the body gives in. The figure kneels in prayer.
Soft sounds begin to release themselves from the throat.
Very soft sounds. These sounds control the gasping body
That aligns itself now. Pause.

Coda: a prayer

(a prayer of transformation)

Man dreams himself
Heaven

He says
Stars
Can I speak?

I want to learn
A new language
To return
The one
I lost.

End of play

On the Act of Regarding Another: Some Thoughts on Live Performance, Silence, and Fragility

Caridad Svich

One: Thinking about Theatre

Let us think now on the nature of silence
On the act of regarding another
That is not the other
But rather another
fellow being on this earth.

Let us think now on the nature of fragility
Or rather, say, the feelings
that are conjured when words such as 'tenderness, weakness, frailty'
are mentioned in relationship to a theatre experience,
and how, in effect, in the theatre
sometimes such frailties are indeed illuminated,
and how at others, oftentimes, buried deep
in the noise and din of the loud, the known, or the 'look at me' vibe
that is often called 'showmanship.'

Let us think now on the nature of darkness,
Which is sometimes mistaken for bleakness
And/or made abject in our regard of theatre work.

So much sadness in this and that play, in this and that show. It is too much to bear.
Please, do not overwhelm, the audience may say.
I come to the theatre to forget. I come to the theatre to escape.
I come to the theatre because my friend said I should come
But really, really I would much rather be at home watching Hulu or Vudu instead.

How long is the show?
Is it 90 minutes?
Oh good. Can we have dinner after? Drinks?

Is it three hours? Five hours?
Is it an event?

Oh, I like events.
I like being seen at events.
Let's make sure we have booked the event.

But what happens when theatre is not an event,
When theatre is not AT you,
Or even generating a buzz
Or even 'found' by the media?

What happens when theatre is,
simply is,
And does ask you to regard
Once again, truly regard, as an act of contemplation,
The fellow beings on this earth,
And reflect upon what it means to be human
At one (or not) with nature?

What happens when theatre is 'hidden?'
When it is in your living room?
Or sitting round a table?
Or just me and you here in this space?

Two: Thinking about Immersion

Much is made and written about
Interactive, digital theatre and the future of immersion.
Let's put the audience to work.
Let's make the passive creatures move
And BE in the Theatre with US!

All good.
All fun.
All in good time.
And sometimes, rather effective.
Certainly not new. Promenade theatre has been around for centuries.
It is simply making a return. In its own way.

Except many times I think about how
so much of the immersive theatre experiences
I have been part of as an audience member

Are designed for able-bodied citizens
And rather ignore, and dare I say, discriminate quite openly
By virtue of staging, design and structure of the event,
Non-able-bodied citizens and/or the frail or elderly.

Is theatre ONLY for those designated as 'able?'
Do we leave everyone else out of the party?
Does it become inconvenient to design a show with interactivity in mind
Without considering ALL of the variables?
Do we allow some people in and not others?
Who is allowed in our theatre?
Who gets to play on stage and in the audience?
The game cuts both ways, you see.
Or should I say ALL ways.

Three: Thinking about Adrian Howells

Performance artist Adrian Howells took his life this year on 16 March 2014.
He had struggled with depression his entire life.
His sad end generated a shock in the community.
He had made it to the age of 51, after all.
The struggle would seem to have been conquered somewhat by virtue of age and experience.
But, well, none of us can know the intimacy of despair
And how it strikes upon a person to such a point that ending seems the only way out.

In the days after his passing, what colleagues most often remarked about Howells was, well, his generosity of spirit,
And yes, his motto, always cheekily said by him, 'It's all allowed.'

One of Howell's last pieces *Unburden* (performed at Battersea Art Centre in November 2013)
welcomed the audience into a space lit with candles
And asked that the audience find comfort and open-ness in the space,
Enough trust, in other words, to unburden themselves
Of their feelings of anxiety, trouble, and so forth.

In asking that the audience call out their burdens,
The space became heavy with all,
But the audience left the space a bit lighter, a bit freer,

Because the pact between Howell's deceptively simple construction of the event
and its relationship to the audience
Was that the space, the shared space, could indeed hold
All of the burdens
And allow for a feeling of being unburdened to occur.

You could say that the experience of *Unburden* could be thought of as a prime metaphor
For the what of what is theatre:
We walk into a dark space.
We unburden ourselves.
Or we are unburdened somehow by being in the darkness,
and we walk out, at the end of the evening, into the light.

Four: Thinking about Access

Access is not always about money.
Access is also how you invite the audience into the theatre
(be it in a building, outdoors, or otherwise)
How you invite artists into the theatre,
And whether you make them feel at home.

We talk a lot about values in our society.
We take seminars on the key values we need in order to create effective business models.
We take lots of notes.
But really, all of the note-taking in the world won't mean much
If the basics of what we do in theatre practice are not honored.

How do you invite the audience in? And why?
How do you invite artists in? And for how long?
How many gatekeepers are there?
Who gets to play on all sides of the invisible table?
In the US theatre industry, we have spent a good part of the late 1990s and the 2000s
Talking about the edifice complex
And the dangers of being beholden to a building –
The costs of maintenance, filling seats,
and getting the doors open and closed on a daily basis.

It is pretty much a done deal that being beholden to a building
Does not great art necessarily make.
The building can hold the art hostage and its makers as well.

But we rather love our edifices
And somehow keep fooling ourselves into thinking
That upholding the edifice is the name of the game,
When it matters much more
What the hell we are doing inside the edifices,
How we are doing it,
For whom,
And how we sustain healthy relationships
With our fellow citizens and the world.

Five: Thinking about History

I did not know that we made theatre to fill seats.
Bean counter-like.
I thought we made theatre to invite people,
To welcome them into an experience,
To share a ritual,
To have communion,
To break bread and maybe even some wine,
To think,
To regard,
Yes,
To regard one another
And to contemplate the why of why we are in the world
Today, yes, in this moment, in the now
But also, yes, where we have been, and where we may be going.

Theatre-making is record-making.
That is, making theatre is an act of recording history.

I believe this more and more as I make things –
Reflecting the moment, the cultural whats-it,
Whether I mark the page Now or Then,
Whether the subject is ripped from the headlines
Or 'purely' invented.

We are always recording, documenting in our own way
Who we are and leaving traces for the future (in hope)
That someone may remember
If they are able to read the signs we have left behind.

How do we want our theatres to be remembered?
As good seat-fillers?
As something more?

Six: Thinking about the Audience

I do not like feeling as if I a mere seat-filler
When I am in the audience.
I don't say this out of any sense of nobility.
I know theatre belongs to the bawd as much as it does to the church.
But I do think, I do want, every single time, yes,
For the event to matter, somehow, even if it's in a small way.

I don't expect to have a life-changing experience every time I go to the theatre.
It cannot be.
We know this.
It's too hard to do the work, to make the work, to simply put things in motion,
To ask that art be able to cast a spell upon us in such a manner
Every single time.

It's impossible.

In fact, I think I would be rather disappointed if
Theatre was ALWAYS great.
I think I would become suspect of it, and maybe walk away
Even though I have given it most of my life.

What I do expect is for the invitation to be equitable somehow.
Which is hard when you are paying hundred dollars for a seat in a commercial house
Or sometimes even, yes, in a so-called not-for-profit house.
But the economics of all of this is another story.

When I talk about equity, I suppose I mean that the engagement,
The human engagement set in motion
Between the event and myself, and myself in the crowd
Be one that levels the playing field, so to speak:

You are here.
We are all here.
Let's play.

Sounds simple. But many times when I am in the audience
I do feel as if the event is made without any desire to engage at all.

It is as if you have walked into a party
And the host couldn't care less if you were there or not.
And you are not offered much of anything.
And you are not asked much of anything.
You are treated, I don't know, like an object.
An object that has to be there to fulfill some sort of function,
But really, the event could carry on without you,
And no one would really care whether you are there or not.

Okay, maybe the actors would care.
Actors do care most of the time.
But for the sake of this argument, and the nature of such events,
Let's say that 'caring' is not a word that is high on the agenda at such 'parties.'

Now, sometimes parties such as these are, well, intriguing
And curious to go to, and say that you've been.
But being held in contempt is not a feeling that warrants much affection for long.
Just as being held in too much rapture can become suffocating.

You are here.
We are here.
Let's play.

Seven: Thinking about Ethics

Theatre lives in its historical materialist moment as much as it lives in the spiritual realm.
Theatre asks us to regard a subject and a subject position: it asks us to witness
Not merely to look.

We do all sorts of looking all the time.
Our lives are filled with meaningless engagements.
So, you could say that when we come to the theatre, we are looking for meaning.
We are searching for something.
We hope to find it in the theatre.
But really we find it in ourselves after the event is long over.

Theatre paints images and words on our mind

And much effort goes into these paintings by all of the practitioners involved.
Hours and hours of decision-making and creative problem-solving
In order to suss out how to make the most of the laboratory space
So that when the audience is invited, the paintings can evoke meaning
(On many levels and not purely of the cerebral kind.)

Theatre is holding someone's hand, looking at them in the eyes,
Playing with closeness and distance, and through that interplay
Opening up a space for other 'meanings' to occur.

We can talk about values and systems all we like.
We can take notes. We can look at what nifty marketing tools are out there
To keep the business of the business of theatre going.
But the values of theatre have not much to do with spread sheets or time tables
Or whether the lobby has sustained a forty million dollar renovation or not.
The values of a theatre are felt as soon as you walk in –
And here, I do mean, an edifice, if there is one.

Are you greeted?
Does someone say hello?
Are you greeted with a smile?
Or are you made to feel as if you are an intruder?
Is there a place to sit and wait in the lobby?
Do you feel at ease? Or does the space – the waiting area – make you feel nervous?
Are you hustled in and hustled out of the space?
Do you feel as if you would return if there was not an event in the space?
Does the space itself feel like an invitation?

The 'values' of a theatre are in how we treat each other,
How we engage WITH each other,
How we behave toward one another,
And yes, how we regard one another
As not the Other
But fellow human beings
In a space democratic enough to allow
For the big and little of our lives
To be welcomed,
And treated with kindness, respect, honor and tolerance,
And for these words to be used as not mere lip service toward some mission statement
Written long ago, but to be part of the daily doing of a theatre's life.

The theatre that is life. After all.

The Orphan Sea

Caridad Svich

The Figures

The ACTORS play:

The Odysseus chorus – those that cross rivers and seas

The Penelope chorus – those that wait for those who are crossing, and the one who searches for the lover long gone.

The chorus of the city – including the voice of the river, the neighbor, and the voice of the road.

Time: Now. And a memory of times before (mythic time).

Setting: A fluid space, one that can evoke river, road, city, ice floe, and a rock in the middle of the ocean.

Notes on Text and Staging

The play may be cast with as little as five, or as many as nine or more actors.

Although three choruses are listed, eventually ALL choruses are one. The delineation above is to help separate the different types of 'music,' as it were. Text in the play is not differentiated in regards to specific voices. Sometimes Penelope speaks alone, sometimes with chorus. Sometimes chorus is in unison, sometimes individualized, etc. Decisions regarding this should be made in the rehearsal process and should vary, depending on creative team involved in production.

In the first production, there were three actors in each chorus.

The play calls for a light (in spirit) approach, despite (at times) somber themes. The poetry should be handled, in other words, lightly, conversationally (albeit heightened). The space of play should be welcoming, rather than forbidding for the audience.

Movement, gesture, sound-score, and mediation should be part of the staging of this piece. If you read this and perhaps think of dance-theatre, or hybrid theatre, which includes new opera, then that would be a place to begin exploring the gestural world of the piece.

Music to the author's lyrics for 'The desperate song of no access' has been written by Dani Mann and is available upon request, or the lyrics may be re-set by another composer.

Script History

This play was originally commissioned and produced in fall 2014 by the Department of Theatre at the University of Missouri at Columbia, Rhynsburger Theatre (Artistic Director Heather Carver) under the direction of Kevin Brown.

Invocation

(The actors speak with the audience.)

Here
On this earth

There are those that cross rivers and seas
There are those that wait for those that are crossing,
There are those that wait for their lovers to return,
Like Penelope once did for Odysseus all those years ago

Here
on this earth

There are also those who simply live
With the memory perhaps of waiting or having waited
With the memory perhaps of crossing or having crossed

These memories may wake them in the middle of the night
These memories may stir them to dig for their long-lost dead
These memories may make them wander the earth
In search of a time when they sat under the trees
Along the rivers and seas
And bathed in the glow of summer blossoms

Here
On this earth

There are those too who live in the land of wires
Those like us
    Those like us

Who may feel from time to time
That they cannot trust the memories of the past
And must do all that they can to forget
That Penelope and Odysseus were ever here
And that there were/are wars
from which they were/must be return-ed

Here
On this earth

We speak a language plain
But sometimes too a language of sorrow
a language of bones and a language of song

Here
On this earth

Between the Tigris and Euphrates
(from which we have all come)
We make stories across rivers and seas

Some may last a few seconds
Others a lifetime, others may be only dreams
But they are all our stories.

1st Movement: Crossings

1st Prelude

(The following text may be heard (as VO, live, or pre-recorded) in the transition between the invocation and scene one.)

Later
This shivered world
Will speak
In tongues
Made of rock and sky

We will try to learn this language

We will fail
We will try again

Not until later, much later
Will we understand that
This new language
Cannot be learnt
Like other languages we were taught once

Its alphabet is not made of letters
But of other things
That are more like cries
Whispered
In the dark.

One: crossing

(The Odysseus chorus – those that cross the rivers and seas.)

Soft like this we whisper little cries of hope
against those that hold us against its promise
we do not like this word 'hope' but for now it is the only word we have

it is a strange word. We sound it with our mouths: hope.

Its signs are ash
Rippling across an invisible sea

Who made this word? Who gave it meaning?
Why do our fathers and mothers ask us to use it when we cross?

I cannot buy water with hope, Odysseus says
    I cannot buy shelter with hope, the other Odysseus says
        I cannot buy anything without the hope of coin in my pocket, we all says

Use it anyway. It is a useful word. It will yield, our mothers and fathers say

So, we use it
Crackling against our tongues, rebelling against its sign
While inside, we shout: GIVE US ANOTHER WORD

Through the echo of our shout, we see Penelope, as if in a dream
    We see Penelope waiting for us on the other side of the earth
        She has been waiting for years
The dream of seeing Penelope again sustains us
Perhaps we will be return-ed to each other
(one can hope)

We keep crossing
as the soles of our feet bleed across the rocks and stones
Leaving trace of our passage to the coming rain

Two: water/no water

(A dance of rain, and then the Penelope chorus – those that wait for the ones that are crossing.)

I am standing in the rain

I am standing in the rain waiting for my daughter/son, Penelope says
    I am standing in the rain waiting for my brother/sister, the other Penelope says
        I am standing in the rain waiting for my lover Odysseus, we all says

It is a hot day
    A hot day with rain
        And we never have rain

Not like this
    We feel blessed
        We feel a little angry

The rain licks our lips
    Tickles our nose
        Settles into our skin

It distracts us from the waiting
    Because the waiting

For Odysseus to make it across
    Has no date
        Even though we sometimes look at our calendars
        As if they will answer our prayers

Three: earth signs

(The one who searches for the lover long gone is also Penelope.)

Yesterday I dug my hands in the earth
It was cold
Even though the weather, the weather, as we say, was hot

The cold entered my fingers
But I kept digging

In this earth
My lover – also known as Odysseus – once was

I remember
Even if no one else does
Because it was many calendars ago

The ants and worms know my lover's secrets
They have been listening all this time
They have been listening to the bones

In the earth
I dig for kindness, humility, arms

Yes, I dig for my lover's arms
To hold me again

Four: stuff

(The Odysseus chorus – those that cross the rivers and seas.)

Two hundred years from now
Our crossing will not make the headlines
Because all borders will have flooded

The teeming overwhelming-ness of us
Crossing rock, stone, water, fence
Will be the stuff of the morning news at breakfast, if it will be the stuff at all

Two hundred years from now
My brother's great-great-grand sons and daughters
will not remember how it is they came to this land

This will be a matter for the historians to sort out
Or better yet, the philosophers

My brother once pursued a degree in philosophy
Before the laws of violence set in

He once waited for his/our land to heal
From the constant suffering
But it would not stop, and so, he fled
And hoped against hope that the wind would carry him elsewhere
    My brother never studied again
        Two hundred years from now, will we still have philosophers?

Five: electric gardens

(Penelope waits in the garden of the then and now (time before and present).)

At noon in the garden
A kind of light
Shimmering and strange

I, Penelope, reach out
I hold the light in my hands

But it slips away
Onto other hands
bodies
seas

At noon in the garden
I, Penelope, dream of the sea

Figure 7: Performer Dani Mann in *The Orphan Sea* (2014). Commissioned and produced by University of Missouri-Columbia © University of Missouri.

Long ago in Crete and other mythologies we vaguely remember now
The sea was oracle

My mothers and fathers called to it and perhaps used the word 'hope'

Sometimes the garden blooms light
Sometimes the sea harbors ruin
Sometimes the waiting gnaws at my sinews
It is then, yes, that I pray for peace

<u>Six: yesterday</u>

(The Odysseus chorus look across the shivered world.)

Yesterday I, Odysseus, dreamt a world

It was neither glass nor concrete
Instead it was made of open paths and trees
And small islands

You dreamt it with me
You saw it with your eyes
You walked its valleys
You swam its seas
You did not get lost
        (The Penelope chorus responds across the shivered world.)

In our dream of yesterday we imagined a low fire

We let it bathe us in its light
It was warm and soothed our tired skin.

Yesterday, you were my lover, Penelope says
    Brother/sister, the other Penelope says
        Daughter/son, we says

Yesterday we thought dreams of the world were possible
Yesterday you and I
knew nothing except for love

Seven: this world

(The Penelope chorus.)

This world
Asks too much
Surrenders too little
Suffers under the weight

To the extent of which we are exempt from suffering
Someone says

The words echo

(Text scroll of echoed words: 'To the extent of which we are exempt from suffering')

I, Penelope, try to make sense of them
I, the one who digs for her Odysseus in the earth, tries to hold these words in my hands
I do not understand

How can one be exempt from suffering?
It is like saying I will no longer touch
Feel
Anything

I suppose it is possible
To live in such a world
To make believe it is real
To construct it in such a way
As to ward off everything else

I do not know if I could live in such a world
I do not know if I could allow myself to be exempt
Although sometimes, yes, I am tempted, as are we all

Eight: letting go (migration)

(One who has crossed (an Odysseus of the many Odysseus in this world) is seen by the chorus of the city.)

Quiet it seems the path he took across the desert
and later across the river dripping with fear

How many were there besides him it is hard to say
there were many others for whom we, who live in the city,
in the city he once dreamt of,
    in the city where he once promised his love,
do not have/know exact names

but he, this Odysseus, made it across once.
This we know when we looked into his eyes
when we swallowed our pride
when we kept our own fears close in the dead of night

often he will smile
and we do not know if it is a smile of sadness or mirth
we do not ask
we know not to ask

and this has nothing to do with translation
because there are many languages here
and we have learned to speak some of them
though there will always be others
we would rather not learn

too hard

and it is true, some languages are
our brains can only take so many vowels and consonants and symbols
it is much easier, far easier, yes, to let go

Nine: looking

(The one who waits in the garden (Penelope) regards Odysseus in memory with chorus.)

looking at the cross across your chest
    at the star across your neck
        at the emblem you wear under your clothes
        but sometimes can be seen when I see you in the dark

I, Penelope, think of the times we spent
Under the trees brimming with fruit
    And how we studied the stories and myths those before us called Great

Was it a coincidence
That your arms brushed against mine
    That your throat let out a little sigh
        That you wondered if we could live together like this always?

Once there were great wars
And it seemed as if we would never live together
But then one day, after much death, destruction and suffering
Some leaders said we could be with each other again

There have been many wars since the great wars,
Although we will never really know why they were called 'great'
We have been severed from each other several times
But for now, in this memory, let us sit under the trees

Ten: commodities

(The chorus of the city.)

too often we are told our value is measured only by how much we buy

I would like to say to those that say such things
That I am not merely a purchasing agent
That my desires cannot be manufactured
That my wants are not only fulfilled by obtaining a bigger house and a bigger vehicle

I would like to say such things
Although when I do, when I have
The power of my words do not remain in the air for long

Because I have been taught perhaps too well
    And you know this, friend
That I am only worth what it is that I buy in this economy

So many of us here in the city have been taught this that we have come to believe it
You could say it has become gospel

We do not even think about our worth in other terms
    we do not want to
my grandparents say they learned this lesson too
and that at one time they fought to stop this lesson from being taught
they fought with words
and sometimes with rocks and guns
but in the end, they could not stop the lesson because it ruled the world

Eleven: on days like this

(The Odysseus chorus, the Penelope chorus, and the chorus of the city. (This could be VO to movement sequence).)

on days like this
we like to think we can win

the game of life will be ours

on days like this
we sit under the sun and the stars
and dream of progress

sometimes we hold each other close
at other times we stand far apart. at others we are very still
as if our very breathing could give us away

you can be reckless. so can i
it is in our nature. this much we share
perhaps it is what makes us winners?

A friend remarks that the word 'winning' is politically incorrect
We do not know what our friend means
Policies of entire nations have been writ with this word in mind

Perhaps our friend is afraid, perhaps our friend is weak
We pity our friend and offer a shoulder, but she says it is not enough

Twelve: staring at the moon

(The one who waits in the garden (Penelope).)

In other lands I, Penelope,
called you, Odysseus, mine

We were staring at the moon and your body entered me
It was summer

There was a sound from down below
Something we could not recognize
Something peculiar

It seemed to us to be the sound of a traveler
Or at very least someone who had come from very far
And had found themselves here

We laughed
We liked the sound, even if, at the time, we could not put a name to it

Sometimes it is better when things do not have a name
When they are suspended like this, like us, here under the light of the moon

I always think of you the way you were that summer
The way you kept the city in frame
The way you smelled of oranges and jasmine
And the way the traveler let down his/her hair
As the sound of beautiful strangeness enveloped the air

Thirteen: long ago

(The Penelope chorus – those that wait for those that cross – and the chorus of the city.)

A bell rang
I heard it
We all did

It was not loud

But we responded
Because it seemed as if it were inside of us

We called this over time the bell of fear

We came to rely upon it
To make decisions about our laws
And also about how we were to process human beings
from one patch of the earth to another

My daughter/son
    Brother/sister
        Lover
Were processed
After they crossed rivers and seas

They have river stories to tell, and ones about the land, too
They tell us that they also heard this same bell long ago
But it sounded like something else

Fourteen: fourteen stories about the river

(The Odysseus chorus, and the voice of the river.)

The river sweeps us under
Its tendons breaking ours
Its legs binding us

The river doesn't know anything except rage
The river is lousy in bed
The river wants my blood
The river aches for hope, although we do not like to use that word anymore

Sometimes at night the river howls
The river begs
The river cradles happiness

I want the river in my skin
I want the river in my blood
I want the river to let down the flood

    I want the river in my skin
    I want the river In my blood
    I want the river to let down the flood

        I want the river in my skin
        I want the river in my blood
        I want the river to let down the flood.

Flood me a river

Cry me a river
    Let its tears drown me in Penelope's arms again

(And the 1953 song 'Cry me a River,' in Ella Fitzgerald's version, is heard amplified, through the voice of the river as lip-sync.[1]
The Odysseus chorus moves to the song – a choreographed dance of yearning and release.
Perhaps the song mashes up at some point with the chorus of the 2002 Justin Timberlake song with the same title, allowing this dance of yearning to take on another dimension.
the Odysseus chorus should be spent, exhausted, by the end of the dance, spent enough to finally be able to fall into the river and:)

You are my river

Fifteen: words under duress

(The chorus of the city.)

I am often told the river is dry here
That it will, in fact, never come back to life
Even if all of the concrete were to be lifted
Its currents died long ago

When we are walking past the former river
    Here in the city where old river legends line the veins of our streets
We point to it
If we notice it
And we try to imagine what it must have been like
When it was there
When it actually sung of more than decay in this city

When we are driving past the former river
We try to take a picture of it for our friends to see
It is not a very good picture
Because it does not look like much of anything
But we send a caption and we say
See, under the concrete, it was there
It may still be
We will see if we can find a picture from when it was

We use this phrase: from when it was without even thinking about it
Perhaps we do not want to know what it really means
Or who we were all those years ago

Sixteen: from when it was

(The one who searches for the lover long gone (Penelope) and the neighbor.)

    Are you still digging? The neighbor asks
Many days have passed
And my hands are covered in a blanket of earth
I have not reached my lover's arms as of yet
But I do not give up hope that I will find them

    Perhaps your lover is not in this earth, the neighbor says
I do not understand my neighbor's words
My neighbor has lived here as long as I have
My neighbor has seen the same wars

    Perhaps your lover was moved, the neighbor says

What does my neighbor know?
Did my neighbor see something? Did my neighbor help those who speak hate?
Did my neighbor carry my lover's bones to another side of this earth?

    But the neighbor does not respond
My neighbor – whom I have known for far too many calendars –
Simply looks at me – eyes clouded with indifference
A vague word barely forming itself on his lips

    The neighbor walks toward the other garden
The one without dirt, the one littered with trash
Left behind by those from the time known as: from when it was

Seventeen: mouth

(The Odysseus chorus – those that cross rivers and seas in the mouth of the river.)

The mouth of the river rages
This is no time to cross
But we need to do so anyway
Day approaches and we must avoid the sun

We throw ourselves into its mouth
Its thirst feeds ours
For a while we are one

We ride its tongue
We touch its teeth
We rest upon its lips

    We ride its tongue
    We touch its teeth
    We rest upon its lips

        We ride its tongue
        We touch its teeth
        We rest upon its lips

    Soon, soon, Penelope

Today we will win
One of us shouts
The word 'win' lingers in the tide

Did someone hear it?

For a moment we worry unsteady in the mouth

But the river coaxes us, and soon, we are in its larynx
Breathing its signs, dreaming of Penelope…
The shore is in our sight

Eighteen: the river ha

(The voice of the river (amplified, could be gender masked) and the Odysseus chorus – those that cross. An encounter.)

I could break you
I could take you in my arms and sever you

No one will see
No one will confess
No one will claim you

It has always been like this
In stories of hate
But also sometimes in stories of love

I would like to offer you something
So that you will suffer less

Here are my eyes
Here are my hands
Here are my legs

    Here are my eyes
    Here are my hands
    Here are my legs

        Here are my eyes
        Here are my hands
        Here are my legs
Take them
    Do with them what you will
        Make of them a ripe flower

Perhaps then
You will understand that the hollow laughter
You hear along the river's edge
Is nothing more than an ordinary ha

Nineteen: summer blossoms

(Penelope waits in the memory garden, recalling her lover (Odysseus).)

Did you think when we were there,
When we were in other lands near other rivers
That things would change?

You could barely speak the language
But somehow you could read the signs
I, Penelope, was impressed
And I, Penelope, do not impress easily

I asked you then if you had studied before you came
You swore you did not
I did not believe you
But I did not say anything
Because this was a good time
There had been so few, after all, truly good times between us
And I wanted this one to last
Just a bit more

Look at that, you said
As we passed the courtyard
I turned, but I could not see what you wanted me to see
You asked me to look again, closer still
Over there, a little past the stone figure –
yes, of course, summer blossoms
     and summer blossoms fall from the heavens in the garden of memory

2nd Movement: Here/Now

2nd Prelude (theatre)

(The actors address the audience.)

In theatre, they say
People want things
People crave things
People fight to the death

People do bad things and do them well

People rarely get what they want

People point to their neighbors and itch for the kill

People are strange
People are crazy
People make faces
People fail
They fail a lot

Sometimes they fail so much that we love them for their failure

It makes us feel a little better especially when days are gloomy

In theatre, people make love, make war
make everything
And sometimes, sometimes, make theatre

Twenty: when we were together

(All choruses: the city, the ones who wait, the ones who cross, etc.)

in this theatre

I want
Crave
Hunger
Need
Cry
Bellow
Shout
Scream
Die
Love
Beg
Plead
Dance
Sigh
Swoon
Bleed
Ache
Scorn
Offer
Please
Push
Rock
Touch
Cling
Drown
Run
Fall
Grieve
Laugh
Plot
Order
Cede
Claim
Tender

Wonder
Leave

And then return

           (Perhaps now only Odysseus to Penelope.)

Because I must touch you
Once more

Twenty-one: pulse

(The chorus of the city.)

Today they said the dry river was pulsing
Singing
A kind of song
Of lovers wanting to be near each other again

Even people in rooms sitting in desks staring at screens heard this song

Some people wanted to shout
Others wanted to cry
Others did not know what to say
Because they had never heard the story of Odysseus and Penelope
They only knew stories of wars

Some people wanted to lift the river's song into their machines
They wanted to keep the song forever

But the river would not give up its song
The river had other plans

You could say the river was wise. You could say it was selfish

I like to think that the river knows more than all of us
I remember, you see, standing near the Euphrates once
I held out my hands
Its hum and glow washed over me
It was then that I knew a kind of reckoning was possible in this world

Twenty-two: close

(The Odysseus chorus.)

Light the darkened pulse of morning
Washed ashore along the river's song
Siren-bled
I am here
Where are you, Penelope?

(The Penelope chorus.)

The question rages in my mouth
I have become impatient with waiting
You have been gone too long
And what I remember of you may not be enough to…

(The Odysseus chorus.)

The city is wide
As wide as the sun
As wide as the wars that have broken these lands

I ache for your touch
I beg your benevolence
I reach out my arms in the still-beating air
Where are you, Penelope?

(The Penelope chorus.)

The question gnaws at my sinews
I do not want to think about you anymore
I do not want to know you are here
If you, here
Will you be here
Are you my lover gone?

(The Odysseus chorus.)

I do not know myself
If this me is the same me who kissed you last
I am perhaps disguised in some other flesh

In some other bones that sing of the same sorrows
But I need you all the same
Please, Penelope

                (The Penelope chorus.)

His words echo across the river
Sting the broken land
I shout to my sisters: what blessed curse is this?
To love the love that knows no tomorrow
Only yesterday and now, now…

                (The Odysseus chorus.)

Now the tide of daybreak
The anguished holler craving
Your tongue
Your legs
Your arms
In my arms

                (The Penelope chorus.)

Standing against the splintered skyline of the city
You meet me

                (The Odysseus chorus.)

And I kneel before your eyes.

Twenty-three: here (arrival/return)

(Odysseus chorus and Penelope chorus.)

Today
We spoke in signs
Of forgiveness

After you crossed
    After we stood in the rain
        After the earth sent its signs
            After what felt like two hundred years

Mouths shorn of thirst
Because you were here

In this world again
Or simply, in this world

I wanted to give you things
Offerings from memory

    A wooden spoon
        A flower pot
            A plate of blue

But you said. Odysseus said:
Not now
It's okay
I am full
I have too many things
I don't need anything, actually
I think I will just sit for a while

And we said, I, Penelope, said:
Of course

Because we understood
And remembered too what it was like to sit under the trees
Even if these were not the same trees from the time known as: from when it was

I wanted to give you the river's sheen
As a gift for your constancy

You were looking at me
The way lovers once did in other lands in summer
While travelers found their way

And truth is, although I didn't know how to say it,
Although I didn't know how you would take it
I was glad you were here
And that I, this Penelope, didn't have to wait anymore
Like that other Penelope once did in those old wars we read about once
You, Odysseus, are here and This theatre is ours.

Twenty-four: this room

(Odysseus and Penelope make love. We see them in their rooms of love, as if suspended in the air. The rooms of the Odysseus and Penelope chorus mirror each other. Text could be VO to movement sequence.)[2]

This room of ours tenders its love

Its walls breathe passion
Its floor whispers intimacy

I never knew this room would be mine/ours again
I never thought the river would/could lead me here

Sometimes the room reminds me of when
We gave away our freedoms
To seek others

Sometimes the room reminds me of when
We rocked each other to sleep

Your arms hold me in winter
Just as they once did in summer

Your language sits on my tongue
As it once did when we were young

The emblems you wear are old and worn
But I cherish them still
Because they have survived all wars

Tonight we will make this room
One of promise

You will give me your body
And nothing will sever us

Not even
Our own desires

Twenty-five: calling

(Odysseus and Penelope make a request to the world from their rooms of love.)

And if they call us
Tell them we are not here
    Tell them we have gone
        Tell them we do not wish to see anyone else right now
Save for each other

Is that too much to ask?

The world can wait. Can it not?

It has been years, after all, since I have seen you
    Since we have seen each other

We need this time together
    In this room
We need to awaken our bodies again to beauty

The scar on your left thigh
    The scar on your breast
The tattoo on your ankle
    The way your nipples rise and fall
When we draw close

This is what we see now
    In this room of desire
In this room where waiting once reigned

I caress your cheek
    I cradle your body
I surrender to no one

Because this time is ours

And when they come calling
When they knock on our door
Even if they do so with guns
We will at least have had this time again

Before the river swallows you once more in its arms

                                                 (Interval.)[3]

3rd Movement: Stories

Twenty-six: we were told stories of love

(The Odysseus chorus and Penelope chorus watch the film of Penelope and Odysseus traveling through the city.)[4]

Along the dry river you see here in this picture

You see here
When we walk past the old construction site

The lovers used to live
So the legend goes
(although it is not a legend written in any official book)

The lovers would float along the river
Until they reached the other side of the city
(or was it the other side of the earth?)

Look here
Along the dry bed cracking through the concrete
You can almost see the outline of their bodies

The one who waited
The one who crossed rivers

The one who knew languages
The one who was impressed
The traveler, orbiting in peculiar-ness.
Meeting perhaps another traveler along the way
And the one, like me, who had a brother who wanted to study philosophy
But whose life took a different turn
Due to laws outside his/her power

If we trace these outlines carefully
If we float along the dry river
We could be these lovers again

(All of the choruses.)

We could be parent to daughter/son
    Brother to sister
             Husband to husband

                Husband to wife
                    Wife to wife
Human to human

There are, after all, so many different kinds of love
In the bones of this dry river

Some even speak of the one between a person and their country
Or countries they call their own

Because at day's end, we have all come from somewhere
Between the Euphrates and the Tigris

And if you don't believe this,
Then go there,

Stand next to the Euphrates
Stand next to the Tigris

While you still can
While you are still able

When no one's looking
Or standing guard

And Listen to the souls floating in their/our histories
And tell me then
If you do not recognize your blood

The Orphan Sea

Twenty-seven: earth shiver

(The one (Penelope) who searches for the lover long gone finds the lover (Odysseus).)

This morning I found my lover upon the earth
After years of digging
After weeks of being told perhaps the body was no longer here
After days of refusing to believe my lover would never be found

It was early
The sun was beaming
I was a little hung-over from the night before
The buzz of sweet wine on my lips

Uncommon of me to drink
Well, over-drink
With wine, no less
But there you have it

Figure 8: Performers Lynette Vallejo and Alex Givens in *The Orphan Sea* (2014). Commissioned and produced by University of Missouri-Columbia © University of Missouri.

With the blaze of sun against my skin
I walked unsteadily toward the dirty grass
When suddenly there was my lover
Stretched out upon the earth

Whispering to me?

At first, I thought it was the drink
It was all due to the drink
And that my lover was not there at all
But as I drew closer
It was clear
This body was my lover's body
These bones were my lover's bones
This history was mine

Earth shivered my lover to me
Earth had listened to my cries after all this time

I wanted to say thank you
Thank you
Thank you
To the earth

But on this morning of sun, I had no words

Twenty-eight: in the silence

(The Penelope chorus faces the Odysseus chorus.)

In the silence of
Your stare
Across the room of many rooms
Your want
Pressing against my flesh
Your everything
Here
Like the pulse of rain

Hold me, you said
As if whispers were all

And I, too drunk for reason,
Did as I was told

Your heart in my mouth
Your stomach in my arms
Your sex in mine

    Your heart in my mouth
    Your stomach in my arms
    Your sex in mine

        Your heart in my mouth
        Your stomach in my arms
        Your sex in mine

Like then
Back then
In times of old wars
When we held each other close, too close,
Because we knew nothing else,
Even if through it all, Yes, we questioned love

Twenty-nine: other stories

(The choruses of all.)

Other stories will be told
About who we are
And who we have been
It is always so in history

But for now, let us tell our own stories

To some they will be trivial
To some they will seem too full of technology

To some they will simply be less stories
Than something else – some other things with scenes and moments from life –
And these other things might be called portraits
Or maybe they will be called cave paintings
Or maybe they will be called images painted on tapestries and vases
Or maybe they will be made of silver spools called film
Or invisible spools we call media

media material
is that what our lives are?

Please, let not our lives be merely media material

Because, well, I still have a fondness for cave paintings
And those stories told first
Before words became a means to tell

Please, forgive me, I will say
As I approach my brother/sister
If my stories are not ready-made material

But my life/our life is not ready made

If it were, we wouldn't be on this earth
Living how we live
Holding out our hands to the river

4th Movement: Geographies

3rd Prelude

(The actors address the audience.)

Here between the Tigris and the Euphrates
We are always
Current-bled
born to histories
craving what will never be ours

your territory will be mine, we will say
will we even know why we are saying these words?
Or are we merely repeating what someone taught us once?

How many lessons do we carry in our bodies?

Lesson one: this is mine
Lesson two: we will make it ours
Lesson three: we will not listen
Lesson four: we will be happy at whatever cost
Lesson five: we will never know the meaning of happiness
Although we will write many books about it

Lesson six: your lessons are not my lessons
Lesson seven: on this day, we will grant you some freedom
Lesson eight: on this night,
we will burn your brother/sister in retribution for a crime done by others
Hundreds of years ago

Lesson nine: we wait in your arms, as if we were lovers
Lesson ten: we will make a movie about what we don't know
Lesson eleven: we will screen this movie to the world
Lesson twelve: we will wait for awards
Lesson thirteen: we will ask that all representations of reality be true and accurate
Lesson fourteen: we will forget the meaning of theatre

Lesson fifteen: we will promise to be good
Lesson sixteen: we will lie
Lesson seventeen: we will be the best liars ever
Lesson eighteen: we will be the best lovers ever

Lesson nineteen: we will learn to forgive each other
Lesson twenty: we will try again to learn to forgive each other
Lesson twenty-one: we will pray to the gods
Lesson twenty-two: we will wait for prayers to be answered
Lesson twenty-three: we will grow tired of waiting
Lesson twenty-four: we will shout: your territory is mine
Lesson twenty-five: we do not know this lesson

Thirty: waking

(The chorus of the city. Now, after time has passed, after Penelope and Odysseus have been together for a while again.)

waking to the sound
of planes shot down
two hundred some deaths
fuselage in flames

waking to the sound
of another car bomb in the market
fifty wounded, several dead
they are still sorting through the wreckage

waking to the sound
of a person praying on the water
while an oil rig rises up on another shore

waking to the sound
of burning gas shot toward the sky
every day now
24 hours a day
While we cannot sleep
Do not sleep
Do not even try

Waking to the sound
of your passion
Against the rise of the river
Waking to
dreams of the sea
Blue waves cresting against the horizon

I want your tongue

Thirty-one: the other day/the waiting

(Penelope and Odysseus look at the map of the earth.)

The other day the digital map
Pointed me south
I followed its motion
I trusted its veracity
    (Google Map window)

I have become somewhat committed to the concept of truth and accuracy in all things
Even though this is impossible
Especially in theatre, But I try anyway
Because when all privacies, most privacies have been stripped,
Truth and accuracy
Or what some call now 'transparency' may well be all we have
To understand where/who we are

The map points me to your cities, to our villages
To the restless tides of rivers crossed by many
And further still… to coordinates heretofore unseen/known

A dusty road
    A lonely ice floe
        A bruise of rock

The digital map waits for me/us to choose
The waiting is not unlike the waiting for you to return all those years ago
I close my eyes, as if I were a child again, and say: take me there

Thirty-two: a bruise of rock

(Penelope (the one who lost the lover) and Odysseus (the lover gone) on the rock.)

We are upon a rock, you and i
It is the color of a bruise
Out there, there is what looks like a sea
Although we do not trust our eyes so much these days
We have learnt some lessons, after all

The rock holds us well
Despite its crevices
It may have been Prometheus' rock once
It may hold his stories of fire and no rain
Or it may simply be rock
And us
And sea

That's okay
Because we have a backpack
And in it we carry the world
Look

And we do, we see the world… and then…

This is another lesson we have learnt well

Upon this rock
I offer you my loyalty
I offer you my trust
I offer you the greater good of the earth

I offer you everything I have
Which isn't much

But perhaps it will be enough
To let us travel
beyond this rock
To help us bridge the seas

Thirty-three: the ice floe

(Penelope and Odysseus are on the ice floe.)

We are not so good on the ice
We fall a lot
We do not have the proper shoes
We do not have the proper gear
We are not made for ice floe weather

And so, we imagine we live in a hut

And by imagining it, we make it

(Penelope and Odysseus draw the hut – a projected drawing in the air.)

Here in this hut on the ice floe
We seem to be in another story
Although this one is also one of survival

Call it the hut of realism
Call it the hut in the center of a once-village
Now enveloped in ice
Or call it merely a hut
To keep us warm

The ice floe is nestled on a blanket of blue ice
In it we make a life

The hut holds our children
Our dreams
Our stories told at bedtime

We write in this hut
Stories of being left
Of being forgotten
Of being those no longer thought about
By modern civilization

We use the word 'modern' as it might have first been used once:
Full of wonder and the thrill of progress

Modern

We miss being wired to the world
Because here, in this hut, there is no access

(And all of the choruses are seen, perhaps too in their huts on their respective ice floes. They sing:)

'The desperate song of no access'

AT FIRST, WE PANIC
WE BECOME DESPERATE
WE DO NOT KNOW WHAT TO DO WITH OURSELVES
WE CANNOT COMPLETE THOUGHTS
WE CANNOT BE STILL
WE CANNOT EAT
WE CANNOT DO ANYTHING
WE ARE USELESS
FUTILE BEINGS

WE ARE USELESS
FUTILE BEINGS

WE DO NOT KNOW WHAT TO DO WITH OUR HANDS
OUR HANDS ITCH
OUR HANDS MOVE
OUR HANDS TRY TO DO SOMETHING OTHER THAN…

OUR HANDS IMAGINE BEING WIRED TO…

BUT OUR HANDS HAVE NO IMAGINATION

WE ARE USELESS
FUTILE BEINGS

WE ARE USELESS
FUTILE BEINGS
    WITHOUT WIRES

WE ARE DEPRESSED
WE ARE HOPELESS
WE ARE LIKE DEAD THINGS

SITTING ON THE COUCHES OF OUR HUTS
EVEN THOUGH THEY DO NOT HAVE COUCHES

WE SLACK
WE SLEEP
WE DO NOT CLOSE OUR EYES

WE STARE INTO SPACE
WE BLAME EVERYONE FOR EVERYTHING
    EVEN ANIMALS AND PLANTS

WE ARE USELESS
FUTILE BEINGS

WE ARE USELESS
FUTILE BEINGS

WE LASH OUT
WE ARE SULLEN
WE ARE LIKE ANIMALS
WE POUNCE

WE DO NOT KNOW WHY

WE DO NOT KNOW WHAT TO DO WITH OUR HANDS
WE DO NOT KNOW WHAT TO DO WITH OUR EYES
WE DO NOT KNOW WHERE TO LOOK
BECAUSE NO/THING IS TELLING US WHERE TO LOOK

WE MISS OUR THINGS, OUR GADGETS, OUR BEAMS OF LIGHT

WE MISS THEM AS IF THEY WERE THOSE WHO HAVE PASSED
BURIED SOMEWHERE
ASH

WE MOURN
WE GRIEVE
WE ARE ON THE EDGE OF ALL THINGS

WE ARE USELESS
FUTILE BEINGS

WE ARE USELESS
FUTILE BEINGS

WE STARE AT THE WALLS OF OUR HUT
WE BECOME DEPRESSED

WE CONTEMPLATE SUICIDE

…

         (The song ends.)
And then after some time, in the hut,
In the land of no wires
In the land of no/things

We begin to regard each other
As we have perhaps never done
When we lived in our other lands in our other lives

…

I begin to see your smile
And the way it changes every time, reflecting something different about your soul

I begin to see how our children wake to the world
Each day, a new beginning
Each day, a new story to be told
I/we begin to listen, truly listen, to the world

Even here, on ice
The world sings

         And we listen to it for a while.

Thirty-four: the dusty road (a road movie)

(Penelope and Odysseus are on the road.)

Hours now we have walked along the dusty road
It has been a lesson in living
(or so we tell ourselves)

So far we are doing well
(or so we think)

Would you like an apple?
Would you like a pear?
Would you like my kiss flush against your lips?

We ask questions to keep going
We imagine fruit from trees landing on our laps
Poverty eradicated from the earth

We touch the ground
We kiss it

And they do

We ask it to welcome us again
(despite what we have done/may have done in the past)

We kiss it again

And they do
The road speaks to and alongside them

The road looks at them/us
The road thinks this is a fine day for traveling
The road wants nothing to do with trespassing
The road waits for them/us to go elsewhere
But they/we do not know another road
Right now this is all we/they have

After all, we have suffered through rock and ice
And the road, dusty as it is, by comparison, seems the best of the lot

Better than bruised rocks and ice floes and huts

If we had our lives to live over
We would choose the road

Yes

We kiss the earth again

And they do

The road laughs
The road has other plans
The road taunts them/us:

No bellies, no eyes, no waking sounds here, the road says
You want this
I will give you more dust

(A dust storm occurs. The storm is expressed through an extended movement sequence that may involve all of the choruses. The storm is propulsive and hurls all across the space. The dusty road is relentless. But after a while, after waging its little war against all, the storm is over, and, yes, they are left.)

After silence, after dust filled,

We rise
We look around
We ask each other

Would you like to go on?

Yes.

Thirty-five: a summer's day

(Penelope and Odysseus are back in the city.)

On this summer's day
I cannot think how it is we got here

We walked

Yes
But really…

(did we?
Or was it the Google Map?)

And you smile
    And you make faces
        And you try not to be too serious

After all, you remember the rock and ice and how the dust…

Sometimes you make these choking sounds
But you say it is nothing
It is merely the price paid for being here again
With our things

And oh how we missed them
Although now we do not look at our wires and couches and walls
Quite the same
They are things. That's all.

And sometimes, yes, they govern us,
But not for long
Not like before

We know better now
(or so we think)

We will soon forget
Because that is the way of all things

But for now
We will make the most of these summer days

The Orphan Sea

5th Movement: Remains

Thirty-six: you are (alphabet)

(Penelope and Odysseus and choruses, years later.)

You are my letter

In this letter I write

In this letter I will write
After I am gone

You are my alphabet
Brother/sister
    Daughter/son
        Husband/wife
            Husband/husband
                Wife/wife
    Lover
Human

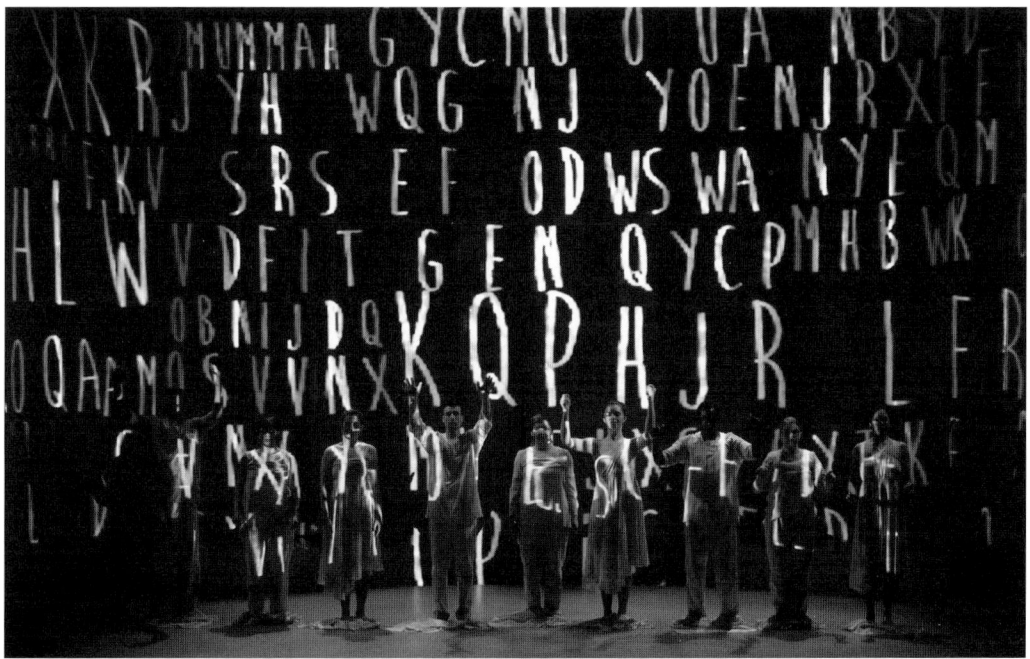

Figure 9: Performers Michael Bayler, Katie Hoy, Courtney Wagner, Randy Hussey, Alexandra Raffini, Dani Mann, Alex Givens, Shelby Gronhoff and Lynette Vallejo in *The Orphan Sea* (2014). Commissioned and produced by University of Missouri-Columbia © University of Missouri.

You are the stuff of my days
Here
In the waking world

Your alphabet is made of letters and signs
Your alphabet is fire water and sometimes plumes of smoke
Your alphabet is a fast sharp slap of rain

Your alphabet is a scroll across the earth
Which I transcribe with my hands
And sometimes with my tongue
And sometimes with my sex

Your alphabet renders me
Flesh

Across your body I will rewrite you, dear one
Because it may be all I can do
When we are both gone

Thirty-seven: the rose (video)

(After everything, the earth speaks of a rose. The italicized text should be scored to video.)

From small beginnings
The rose rises
Pushes through sand
Asks no names

You are
We are
Is all it says

And from small beginnings
We go forth

The children of those who have passed
    The children of those that knew rock, ice, road
        And (the world of) wires

*

(Shift now to live and all of the choruses....)

Close-up:
I am looking at a portrait of the city
The city is ruin
And upon it we have been building
Again

Beautiful things

Although we fear our new houses will not last long
Because we know history
We recall it in whispers and cadences of song
And it has taught us some things

Video.

We are past movie versions of the post-apocalypse
We know that that trend is dead
Yet we still wonder when and how
the destruction of everything became
the elevator pitch to end all elevator pitches

and how some people (with so-called power)
thought imagining a post-apocalypse
was the best way to cope
with the irreality of the Then/Now

Video.

In Greece (and other countries) we seek to pay our debts
We ransack what's left
We ask our old prophets
What the ruins can teach us

It isn't long before
The square becomes filled
With the voices of the young
And old too
And the in-between

Calling for

Reparations
    Equity
        A bit of kindness

We wait for answers

But equity, you see,
Seems hard to find

It must be negotiated
It must be considered
It must be debated
It must be held up to courts of law and enterprise

It is topic
And soon, topic becomes overtaken by other topic

And we are
Video.

1st Coda:

Thirty-eight: us

(The choruses of all. This entire scene is spoken in unison.)

Us here
Wanting
Craving
Beating

Our hearts
Waiting for the world

Not even waiting

Driving it to…
Do what we want
NOW

But we cannot

We know this

And yet
We try
Against all reason

Because sometimes
We can't help ourselves
Because you sit there
At the bar
At the café

You look at me
And at that moment
I want you

And there is no time
Except ours

We will do anything
To get what we want

To NOT surrender

To NOT become
Video.

…

Despite all lessons

We:

The one who crossed the river
    The one who waited
        The one who found the lover upon the earth (after all that time)
           The one who speaks to travelers
               The one who was in other lands once/now
The one who lives in Cretan mythologies
    The one who is documented
Undocumented
From many lands
From this land
From this city
From that village

We
WANT

And even though we already went through ice, and rock and road
We still want

…

Look

Look at the way we look at each other

Can you blame me
If I still want you?

We have hundreds of love songs on our brains
We are in a long line of songs told
Have a drink

Yes
Now

For it is
The drink of life

2nd Coda:

For the audience

(The actors address the audience.)

They say when you walk into a place you have never been
The first thing you do is look for what is familiar
You crave comfort
You want to be re-assured
The same way you are re-assured when you eat the same meal you ate before
Or remember fondly from childhood

This is no different
You want me/us to re-assure you
You want to make sure nothing bad will happen

Listen.

It will be okay.
Everything will be okay.

No harm will come to you here

Isn't that something?
In this world?

So, I ask you

Why don't you tell me, then, about what has happened to you in your stories of love,
In your stories of crossing rivers and seas,
Even the ones we may think of as orphaned?

Tell me your stories.

Let us talk with each other.

End of play

Notes

1. 'Cry Me a River' is a torch song written by Arthur Hamilton. First published in 1953. It was made popular by singer Julie London, who recorded it in 1955. Ella Fitzgerald's recording for Verve Records was in 1961. Frank Sinatra's version is also an option here.
2. VO could be live spoken by the chorus of the city.
3. It is preferred if an interval is taken here.
4. This film could have the feeling of a video diary, something quite DIY, local in its quality. This could also be a live film performed by Odysseus and Penelope – the outlines of the city projected onto their bodies.

Notes on Contributors

Dr. Kevin Brown is an Assistant Professor of Performance Studies and Digital Media in the Department of Theatre at the University of Missouri, US. He has been a producer, director, actor, and designer of theatre for over 25 years. He has published work in *Theatre Journal*; *International Journal of Performance Arts and Digital Media*; *Popular Music Studies*; *Popular Entertainment Studies*; *Journal of Religion and Theatre*; *Puppetry International*; and *Malaysian Studies*. His book *Karaoke Idols: Popular Music and the Performance of Identity* is available from Intellect and University of Chicago Press.

Pedro de Senna was born in Rio de Janeiro, where he started performing in 1993. After obtaining a degree in Graphic and Product Design at ESDI, Rio de Janeiro, Pedro took an MA in Theatre: Text and Production at University of East Anglia, Norwich. He has worked in many areas of the performing arts both in Brazil and in the United Kingdom, from set design to acting, from playwriting to leading workshops with refugees. He currently lives in the United Kingdom, where he is Senior Lecturer in Contemporary Theatre at Middlesex University.

John Moletress is a multidisciplinary artist who collides the cerebral and the visceral in performance through collaborations with artists of mixed disciplines, cultural backgrounds, and intentions of artistic expression. He is founding director of force/collision ensemble.

Dr. Theron Schmidt works internationally as a writer, teacher, and performer. He has published widely on contemporary theatre and performance, participatory art practices, and politically engaged performance. He is a founding co-convener of the international Performance Philosophy network and assistant editor of *Contemporary Theatre Review*.

Caridad Svich received a 2012 OBIE Award for Lifetime Achievement in the theatre, a 2012 Edgerton Foundation New Play Award and NNPN Continued Life Fund rolling world premiere for *Guapa*, and the 2011 American Theatre Critics Association Primus Prize for her play *The House of the Spirits*, based on Isabel Allende's novel. She has won the National Latino Playwriting Award (sponsored by Arizona Theatre Company) twice, most recently in 2013 for her play *Spark*. She has been short-listed for the PEN Award in Drama four times, including the year 2012 for *Magnificent Waste*. Among her other key works are *12 Ophelias; Any Place But Here; Alchemy of Desire/Dead-Man's Blues;* and *Iphigenia Crash Land Falls on the Neon Shell That Was Once Her Heart (a rave fable)*. She has also adapted for the stage novels by Gabriel Garcia Marquez, Julia Alvarez, and Mario Vargas Llosa, and has translated nearly all of Federico Garcia Lorca's plays as well as work from Mexico, Cuba, and Spain. Seven of her plays are published in *Instructions for Breathing and Other Plays* (Seagull Books and University of Chicago Press, 2014). Five of her plays re-imagining ancient Greek tragedies are published in *Blasted Heavens* (Eyecorner Press, University of Denmark, 2012). She has edited several books of theatre and performance, among them *Innovation in Five Acts* (TCG, 2015). She is alumna playwright of New Dramatists, associate editor of *Contemporary Theatre Review* (Routledge, UK), contributing editor of *TheatreForum*, and founder of NoPassport theatre alliance and press (www.nopassport.org).